ECKANKAR:

Compiled Writings
Volume I

PAUL TWITCHELL

ECKANKAR: COMPILED WRITINGS
VOLUME I

Printed in the U.S.A.
ISBN 0-914766-26-0

For a free catalogue of other books printed by Illuminated Way Press please write:

ILLUMINATED WAY PRESS
P.O. Box 82388
San Diego, CA 92138

TABLE OF CONTENTS

ECKANKAR
Ancient Science of Soul Travel

A man who had learned one of the techniques which I give in my workshops on ECKANKAR, the ancient art of Soul travel, reported it was not what he expected it to be.

"It came so easily," he reported. "I did exactly as you instructed, then I heard a sound like the popping of a cork, and found myself on the ceiling looking down upon my body on the bed.

"I had no body, just a pair of eyes like that of a camera, and the knowledge of what was happening. It wasn't at all frightening!"

The experience of this man is similar to that of many who have studied ECKANKAR, the ancient science of Soul travel, under my instructions.

Many have accomplished this supernormal phenomenon, traveling outside their fields of human consciousness, by study and research of the techniques involved. Some during workshops on ECKANKAR that I have given around the country, others by the courses which I teach via the mails.

One student who learned quite well the techniques of ECKANKAR, reported how he could watch the traffic flow while driving to work each morning. "It used to be that I would have to get out of the body and travel ahead to see what the traffic was at a bad intersection several miles ahead," he said.

"But now I do not have to do this. Having the ability to project myself into the higher areas, I no longer travel, but have the perception of knowing.

"I can now put myself on a hill overlooking the highway,

1

move anywhere if needed or just know what the traffic is going to be ahead."

This is true, for we are not dealing with the astral body here nor the mental, for Soul goes far beyond the lower planes. Astral travel is a limited way of traveling, while Soul travel is limitless. It is a feat within itself and not many are doing it.

This student's experience has been proven time and time again by my own training. Soul travel is concerned with the lower worlds while the astral body cannot go beyond its own plane. Soul travel is dealing with the unit of awareness that we know as Soul. It has the ability to move wherever it wishes, has perception, knowingness, a viewpoint, that is the ability to see three hundred and sixty degrees — in other words, it can see from all directions simultaneously. It has perfect freedom.

The astral body does not have any of this type of freedom, only one vision of seeing, that is about one hundred and eighty degrees, similar to the physical sight. It can travel only in the astral world and no farther. It also has the chance of being pulled back with the other bodies of man into another incarnation many times over.

Several years ago while traveling through the Cascade mountains in western Washington, on a long trip home by car, I was fatigued and impatient to finish the journey. While traveling behind a slow moving truck up a high pass, I fianlly decided to pass the truck and started pulling over the yellow line. Just as I did there was a sudden flash picture of a carload of teenagers coming down the steep grade at a high speed. Swinging swiftly behind the truck, the tires of my car skidded across and went half-over the high embankment.

Instantly I was out of the physical senses like a pair of camera eyes looking at the situation. The reaction was swift for in that moment I could see that a sharp, hard left twist of the wheel could put the car back on the road.

2

It all happened so quickly that my physical senses acted automatically and almost instantly the car was back on safe ground again.

This is one example of the use of the Atma Sarup for practical purposes. The use of the Hindu term is given here to acquaint one with what we call the Soul Body, hence Atma Sarup.

But the ability to project this body at will has served me in other tight places: while hunting for gold in New Guinea, diving for pearls in South America, penetrating the dark mysteries of voodoo rituals in the West Indies, while attempting to scale an Alaskan mountain peak, when lost overboard on a ship in a Pacific storm, and when marked for death by an Indian murder cult.

Soul travel can be done by the study of ECKANKAR the ancient science of Total Awareness, which puts Soul eventually into the secret realm of God. Any student of Soul travel has perfect freedom of visiting any of the inner planes he wishes, visiting the planets in this universe — at his own volition.

It must be remembered that Soul travel is concerned mainly with the movement of this Soul body in the psychic worlds, or those that we call the physical, astral, causal and mental planes to that of the fifth plane — sometimes named the Soul plane. It is the first of those ethereal regions which are the worlds of pure spiritual power.

From there we are in the true kingdom and no longer need movement or travel. Soul is beyond time and space which is existent within the lower psychic planes, the worlds of the Universal Mind Power.

We find that as long as we are in the lower worlds, which are in time and space concepts, we are dealing with travel or movement. When we reach the upper levels, beyond the Soul plane, there are no time and space concepts. Travel is not needed and we are in the state of total awareness, often

3

called Absolute Consciousness.

While in this state we become effortless, and are a part of that called Absolute. We exist in the formless world of pure spirit. Hence we have the power to take shape and assume any form we desire in any world. And because of our very separation from these psychic worlds we are placed in the midst of absolute omnipresence of the Supreme Deity which gives us the ability to assume any form, at any time and anywhere.

Therefore we leave the physical senses, not in the astral form, but in the Soul form, which is the unit of awareness, as said previously. We can take shape on the astral plane, or any plane that is so desired. This is how the high masters of ECKANKAR perform their skill, and many times the body in which they appear to us will be like physical flesh, although their corporeal shape is lying abed some thousands of miles away.

Actually we are working in two fields of awareness: that of movement via Soul travel in the psychic worlds and that of total awareness in the heavenly realm. Therefore we are involved here with two states of being — a limited awareness and a total awareness — but both in the Atma Sarup. But we are not interested in the various bodies of the lower planes — i.e., physical, astral, causal and mental — only that of the Soul body. It projects to any plane desired and takes on the form of that particular dimension, as the astral body on the astral plane, mental body on the mental plane, and others on the other varied realms.

My half-sister taught me some of the art of Soul travel before I was able to walk. Most members of my family had this ability. Later she and I went to India to study under Sri Sudar Singh, member of the ancient brotherhood of ECK masters.

He spoke often about his guru, Rebazar Tarzs, the Tibetan spiritual giant, which caused me several years later to start

4

looking for the famed ECK master. He was living near Darjeeling at the time, and appeared suddenly when I was on a mountain trail in search of him.

The meeting was brief and to the point. He gave me the first true encounter with the basic teachings of ECKANKAR. Since then he has appeared to me in all parts of the world, regardless of distance... often to warn me when I was in danger.

At this time he walked me up to the suburbs of the city, but halted to part some bushes to show his physical body lying asleep. Suddenly the body standing beside me disappeared, and the one upon the ground arose brushing his robe. Shaking hands like a Westerner, he said, "I am with you always."

Many people are making the mistake of looking upon Soul travel as that of out-of-the-physical-body. This is a natural mistake for we are taught to believe in astral travel more than any travel outside the human state of consciousness. Astral projection should be the first step to God. But done alone it leads mainly to physical phenomena.

All that the path of ECKANKAR does for anyone is to lead him into the Realm of the Supreme Deity. This alone is the basic goal. If anyone is trying to deal with projection for anything other than this, he is getting into areas of difficulty which create self-delusion and unhappiness.

Of course it should always be used to help others, warn them when in danger, and to give them any spiritual help possible. For example, during World War II, as an officer in the U. S. Navy, I was working with a small crew of men on a twenty-millimeter gun in one of the forward tubs aboard ship. A shell had jammed in the loading and we were trying to unlock it to extract it.

Suddenly my father appeared at my side. "Get out fast," he said. "The gun is going to explode!"

Although he was several thousand miles away in his body,

I was not at all confounded at his appearance for he had done this several times. I leaped over the side of the gun tub shouting at the crew to get out of there. We all must have dropped ten feet to the deck. But as we did the gun exploded, breaking into hundreds of small pieces which would have killed most of us had we not been warned.

Later when visiting home, I asked him about this, but he only smiled. He never spoke about the incident, but we both knew what had happened that day.

ECKANKAR is not very well known. It can be said still to be wrapped in secrecy, as it was during the early ages when only an ECK master would whisper the instructions in a chela's ear. No writings other than my own can be found except in the remote monasteries in Tibet which are heavily guarded.

The sacred writings of ECKANKAR are called the Shariyat-Ki-Sugmad (The Way of the Eternal). This holy scripture is found in those hidden monasteries in Tibet and the spiritual city of Agam Des in the wilds of the western Himalayan mountains.

ECKANKAR is not a religion, philosophy nor occult system, but a doctrine whose modus operandi is to bring about the highest awareness of one's own consciousness and establish within onself the deep significance of the position that one occupies in all places simultaneously.

This brings about many benefits in one's material world, as well as to one's spiritual self, including the arts of self-healing, better economy and control of one's problems, both spiritual and material.

There is nothing wrong with astral projection, except that it is a physical, or better still, a psychic phenomenon. We are still in the lower worlds and not working for total consciousness as we should be doing. If one has not set his aim for total awareness he is wasting his time. An argument in favor of astral projection should be that it gives one the experience of seeing that life extends beyond the physical plane.

ECKANKAR is not to be used to find lost articles, to predict the future for anyone, or put people back together who have been separated because of a lack of good relationship.

However, when one has learned the art of Soul travel, it is natural for him to have developed the ability to read his own akashic records, predict his own future, or to do any of the things mentioned above, including the art of healing and other different things for the universal benefit of others.

The main thing that happens to him is that he becomes purified by reaching certain spiritual planes, and becomes a channel for spirit to flow through to reach others and give them benefits never before known. Once he becomes open for the Divine Spirit to use him as an instrument he will always be under Its protection and never again in want.

Most projection techniques given us by writers dwell at length upon the subject of having us try to project out of the physical into the astral body. This is wrong for it means that we are splitting off the first sheath of the inner bodies to travel inwardly to the astral plane.

This is an unnatural action and could lead to difficulties in the psychic regions, or the lower worlds. We should go out of the physical consciousness in the Atma Sarup, the Soul form, and take on the astral body when reaching that plane. Soul cannot exist on any of the lower planes unless it wears one or all of these bodies, because of the coarser vibrations, unless it wears the particular body which is adaptive to the relative plane it is visiting.

There are four states of consciousness that one must inspect if he is to enter the field of ECKANKAR. These states are: the Human Consciousness, the Psychic Consciousness, the Self-Realization Consciousness or Soul Consciousness, and Total Awareness which is God Realization. I will not take up the definite study of these states here, but will point

7

out briefly that they are defined as follows: the Human Consciousness is the mind or mental state in the physical senses, that which we call the lower negative self. It is always chewing over something, always has physical and mental barriers to surmount.

The Psychic Consciousness is that state in which we are concerned with psychic phenomena in the astral, causal and mental bodies. It is that which we call the upper negative self. It is always working on survival beyond the physical senses; but there is nothing permanent about it.

The Self-Realization state of consciousness is that dimension which Soul reaches to find itself. By finding itself it also gains perfect freedom. It is called the fifth plane by those who follow the path of ECK. Here we recognize ourselves, know who we are, and understand the true goal of life.

The Total Awareness state, or God Realization, is achieved when soul is able to reach the highest realm of all reality. Here it is not in the same field of preference as the lower planes below the fifth plane. Here Soul, that unit of awareness spoken about earlier, is above time and space. Therefore, it never has to move or travel but perceives and knows all things.

Out of my studies I have found that five techniques are about all that a person traveling the path of ECKANKAR needs to know. From these he can select one or two and use them constantly. They are: the astral technique, the mental technique, the dream technique, the trance method, and the direct or Atma Sarup (Soul body) projection.

Practically all people can do Soul travel; but having mothing for comparison they are apt to dismiss it as imagination or shrug it off. But it is comparatively easy to experience out-of-the-body projection under one's own control.

The only factor to keep one from practicing it is being

needlessly afraid something may happen while outside the physical senses. But it is as natural to be in the spirit body as to experience any normal function of eating and sleeping.

One of the simple techniques which I have developed over the years is one called "The Effortless Way."

Just before going to bed at night sit in an easy chair, or on the floor. If you cannot do either of these, then use the couch. Keep the body straight and concentrate the attention on the spiritual eye, the place between the eyebrows, while chanting a sacred word, e.g., AUM, GOD, SUGMAD, or any other one that you might know, inwardly and silently or by chanting softly to yourself.

Hold the attention against a black screen in the inner vision, and keep it blank. This means to keep it free from any mental pictures at all if possible.

If you need a substitute for any mental pictures that might flash into the mind compulsively, place there the image of a saint, a holy man that you know, or your spiritual teacher.

After a few minutes of this there should come a faint clicking sound in one ear, or the sound of popping like a cork pulled from a bottle.

One finds himself standing outside the physical consciousness looking back at the human body in the room. Instead of being in another body like the astral he is like a pair of eyes. He is now ready for a short journey into the invisible worlds.

Usually there will be some entity like a spiritual guide standing by to assist if one should get into any difficulty during the first few journeys. So there is nothing to fear for no harm can come to anyone while outside the physical senses.

When the Atma Sarup is ready to return to the body it slides gently into its physical shell with hardly more than a very slight jolt.

If not successful the first time, try it again, because the

9

technique works. It has done so many times for those who have tried it the first time.

One prisoner in a state penitentiary used this technique, after corresponding with me, for the first time. He wrote, "Suddenly I found myself standing outside the front gates of the prison walking down the road.

"But the sudden movement of myself out of the human body to another area startled me so badly that I almost instantly sprang back into the body. I lay there on my cell bunk wondering what had happened. But after a few times I got used to the idea and can now do it almost at will."

Most persons who have attended my workshops on ECKANKAR over the world have learned to do Soul travel. But so can anyone else who wishes to learn this ancient art of spiritual awareness. . .which will eventually lead him into the ultimate Realm of God.

INTRODUCTION TO ECKANKAR

CAN YOU BE IN TWO PLACES
AT THE SAME TIME?

The woman who met in the auditorium of the Parapsychology Foundation one evening, just before my workshop on ECKANKAR was excited but still a little apprehensive over her first out-of-the-body experience.

"I was sitting in meditation doing exactly what you told me to do last night," she explained breathlessly. "Then I heard this funny sound which went like the popping of a bottle cork and I found myself standing on the other side of the room looking at my body in the chair."

Instantly I knew what she had experienced. It is a spiritual phenomenon rather common to most people who are researching in the field of supernatural reality. A careful study of the case histories of Christian saints and Eastern adepts will prove that it is a living experience which can be brought under control of the operator himself.

My first experiments in the field of Soul travel, being in two places at the same time, came at an age when most children are learning to totter across the room at the coaxing of a loving parent. Most of my family were able to do Soul travel on their own initiative and explore the other worlds.

Sometimes my older half-sister would seat herself across the room from me and call, "Get up and walk over here without moving your body." Whereupon I would proceed to climb out of the physical body and move across to her, tottering as if on human legs, and fall into her lap. We played all sorts of games in our Atma Sarup bodies, the light body as it is called in the Hindu language, e.g., leaping out of the

11

window in the other body, getting on the roof of the house, and pestering the animals around our home. Of course, my stepmother put her foot down on this sort of tomfoolery when she would find out, which wasn't a bad idea at the time, for we had no sense of adult morality which must be part of the modus operandi.

Years later, while in Paris visiting my half-sister who was studying art, I found her seriously interested in an Eastern adept, Sudar Singh, from Allahabad, India, who taught the way to the higher consciousness was via Soul travel. Fortunately the two of us were able to follow him to India and live for a year in his ashram learning much about out-of-the-body traveling.

During the following years, I studied every feasible Soul travel theory known, made some trips abroad to the Orient where I read manuscripts, talked with adepts, gurus and holy men on the subject, and practiced all the techniques which we learned about, just to see what they were like.

After Sudar Singh passed on, I went through a series of studies under various teachers, similar to Meher Baba, who had nineteen during his chela period.

Sudar Singh, who lived in his ashram in India, had the ability to appear to his own people in his Atma Sarup (Soul Body) no matter where they might be. A skill which almost anyone can learn, once he gets the knack of Soul travel, i.e., a number of my students in the Parapsychology Foundation workshop could verify this.

Among my numerous discourses from many gurus in the flesh and those on the inner planes are those taken down when Sudar Singh appeared in my apartment in New York City in his light body, although his flesh self was six thousand miles away in India. This is also true of Rebazar Tarzs, a Tibetan monk, who appears quite frequently in my home. Last fall he dictated a book-length manuscript called "The Far Country." His present abode is near the Hindu Kush range in Afghanistan, where he has lived since the Chinese have taken over his country.

My wife and I arrived on the Pacific Coast where we settled down after wandering around the globe studying spiritual biometrics. I took up teaching a workshop in ECKANKAR at the Parapsychology Foundation as part of my research program, aside from my regular writing career. The workshop has become exceedingly popular and almost every student who attends for at least three times has some degree of out-of-the-body experiences under his own control.

Mainly, I am teaching that ECKANKAR is the main key for unlocking the secrets of the spiritual universe. It is the proof of survival of man after death, for it gives evidence that all things have life beyond this physical plane, including animals and plants. Life reincarnates in millions of physical forms on this Earth plane but these are only the various manifestations by which the SUGMAD manifests ITSELF in the outer world for the physical senses of man to enjoy.

The purpose of ECKANKAR is simply to be able to reach that realm of spirit which is known as the Kingdom of Heaven where IT has established ITS fountainhead in the center of all universes. Hence, the SUGMAD is the modus operandi that we as spirit use as the vehicle to reach our true home again.

The greatest problem with this particular aspect of spiritual phenomenon is that it has received a lot of drubbing at the hands of its critics, and the semantics have become a melange of confusion. Hardly any of those who are able to exteriorize speak the same language. This lack of vocabulary is the reason why many mystics communicate with one another by hand language instead of orally, for language has never been available to describe the wonders that they saw while traveling in the spiritual world.

The basic aspect of ECKANKAR is spiritual freedom, a liberation from the physical body. Once the individual has

13

learned bi-location he is free to come and go as he wishes in the spirit form. When death occurs, he can leave it freely and enter into the spiritual worlds to be with his loved ones who have passed on before him or live where he feels it is best fitted for his spiritual temperament and according to his desire.

As Soul gets nearer the ultimate heavenly world it becomes more individualized. This individualization of the consciousness of the traveler brings a freedom never before experienced. Therefore, where we find security and union with God in the cosmic consciousness state, we find individualization and freedom in the ECKANKAR state. What could be more free than to be able to leave the body by one's own free will and travel to another world to study under some great teacher?

Of course, Soul travel is the answer. It gives all who can master this art the opportunity and the choice of being free and independent of matter, energy, space and time.

Kabir, a sixteenth century Hindu mystic, was accountable for unwrapping the mystery of the art of bi-location. Prior to his day, all knowledge of this spiritual phenomenon was kept secret among those who were highly skilled in it. Rama, the first known saviour of the human race, made his way across Tibet from the northern Himalayas to Persia several thousand years ago. Here he paused long enough to give the secret teachings to that little band of mystics who later became known as the magi, under Zoroaster, the Persian sage. Rama then proceeded to India where he settled down and taught the people that salvation was possible even in one's present life.

In those days the teachings of Soul travel were done orally. No instructions were ever written down and distributed until Kabir, a direct descendent in the line of Rama's spiritual mastership, came here especially for this purpose — to give it out freely to all who wanted it. He taught openly, against opposition which at times became violent enough to seek his life had he been caught.

Since Kabir's time the study of Soul travel has become

14

somewhat an open teaching for those interested, however there is hardly any literature or teachings on the subject. It is still belittled and greeted with disdain from orthodox religions and followers because the emphasis of our times has been to make popular the intellectual senses of the twin doctrines of logic and reason.

From Kabir's day, those who have helped spread the doctrine of Soul travel were mainly the leaders of the Sikh order, especially Guru Nanak, the founder. Others have been the Sufi saints, e.g., Hafiz, Jalal din'l Rumi, Shamus-i-Tabriz, Sudar Singh, St. Anthony of Padua, and the contemporary clergyman, Padre Pio, to name a few.

One of the simple techniques which I have developed over the years is one I call "The Easy Way." Just before going to bed at night, sit in an easy chair or on the floor, back erect, and concentrate the attention on the spiritual eye, that place between the eyebrows, while chanting HU, or God, inwardly and silently. Hold the attention on a black screen in the inner vision, and keep it free from any picture if at all possible. If you need a substitute for any mental pictures flashing up unwantedly, place the image of the Living ECK Master or some saint, or a holy man that you know, in place of them.

After a few minutes of this, suddenly there will come a faint clicking sound in one ear, or the sound of a cork popping, and you will find yourself outside the body looking back at the physical one in the room, and ready for a short journey in the other worlds.

There is nothing to fear for no harm can come to you while outside the body, nor to it when left behind. The Living ECK Master will be standing by, although you may not know it, to keep watch over your progress. After a while the Atma Sarup will return and slide gently into the body with hardly more than a very slight jolt.

If not successful the first time, try it again, for the technique works. It has worked for others.

Most of those in the workshop at the Parapsychology Foundation learned to do Soul travel. So can anyone else who really wishes to learn this ancient art of spiritual phenomenon.

ANCIENT THEORY
CONTESTS EXISTENTIALISM

The riots, freedom marches, obscene behavior and revolt against civil authority by students and junior groups lie in the fact that Existentialism as a philosophy for the sophisticated which sparks our modern rebellion has been a failure.

The washout of this theory of humanistic ideology accepted by university and college philosophy departments as authentic is in the fact it hasn't stood the test of time for its short life since its founder, Soren Kierkegaard, foisted it on the world about a hundred years ago.

Its misfire has left us in a state that brings resentment over any intrusion or interference with our so-called independence and freedom of thought and action.

In its place is an ever popular fad among the minority thinkers called ECKANKAR, which is the ancient science of Soul travel, or what we might call the extended consciousness of the Absolute. Its growth has been phenomenal among the elements revolting against the restrictions of the good society formed by our political leaders, especially for the benefit of the latter.

Youth has always been in a state of rebellion, but in our modern times where everything has gone to the dogs over the socialistic system, things have sure gotten rough. We have been given the good life from the cradle to the grave, leaving adventure for hardly anyone but the astronauts, those who chase UFOs and those who fly the heavens in the space capsules.

ECKANKAR, which furnishes ways and techniques of extending the consciousness to unheard of awareness, is the only answer today for anyone seeking non-conformity and adventure in any aspect of life.

Among those who have kept Existentialism alive since

Kierkegaard published his book on the subject have been Jean-Paul Sartre, Jacques Maritain, Nicolas Berdyaev, Paul Tillich, Karl Jaspers and Frederick Nietzsche, to name a few. Even among them the conflict has somewhat been a contest of whether God existed or not. The anti-Christian doctrines, including Existentialism, have gone far in helping the revolt of junior groups.

The brakes to keep man's mind from progressing have been many, but in these times of confusion we turn again to the ancient concepts of expanding the awareness. Faced with the basic problem that we must again be the free individual, only ECKANKAR can handle the situation and give man his opportunity to extend his consciousness until he is the full being and can benefit by it here and now.

It is done by projection of the consciousness, sometimes called out-of-the-body experience. This phrase is discouraged because too many metaphysicians and occultists call it astral projection, an idea which no one wants to raise, for the extension of awareness as consciousness is the most important instrument in making us free. It is that path we call ECK-Marg, meaning, of course, the path of ECKANKAR.

ECKANKAR is closer to being in its original form than any of the metaphysical theories existing today. It has been handed down by word of mouth from Rama, the first world saviour, who came out of the deep forest of northern Europe, across to Persia, where he paused long enough to give these secret teachings to a few mystics whose descendents were to become the followers of Zoroaster, the Persian sage. Rama proceeded to India where he settled and taught that we could have the experience of reality in one's own lifetime.

Kabir, the sixteenth century Hindu mystic poet, was responsible for unwrapping this ancient science of Soul Awareness for the mundane world. We know it in these modern times as Soul travel, but in those days it was sometimes called Shabda Yoga, but more often ECK-Marg, or what we know as ECKANKAR.

No written instructions were ever put down on palmyra leaves or even stone tablets until Kabir, who was a direct descendent in the line of Rama's spiritual mastership, proposed to distribute freely to all who wanted to know about ECKANKAR. He proceeded to give out all the hitherto secret teachings openly despite all opposition which at times became so violent he would have had his throat sliced if caught.

Many others have helped spread the doctrine of Soul travel, the extension of conscious awareness, e.g., the old Persian literary sages, Hafiz, Firdusi, Omar Khayyam and Jalal din'l Rumi, who was a great intellect in his day. He held professorships in four universities at the same time. These included law, literature, religion and philosophy. If extended awareness makes one versatile, Rumi is the best example we can find in this field.

Among the Western saints who were adept at this phenomena were St. Anthony of Padua, St. Bernard and a few others, including a contemporary churchman, Padre Pio, a living stigmatist, and Capuchin, at San Giovanni Rotono, Italy.

ECKANKAR, which is the ancient art of Soul travel, has a greater advantage over Existentialism. It is concerned with the universal and the individual, while its opposite is concerned only with intellectualism. In other words, we have here two opposing philosophies; ECKANKAR working directly under spirit, while its opposite, Existentialism, works with the intellectual senses.

ECK is not concerned with moral issues because it is known that as the conscious awareness is extended into the other planes of reality that the habits which are useless for survival will drop away. Nothing which is not of value to us will remain, e.g., if smoking too much, this habit either will drop naturally or come into balance.

Existentialism is a philosophy of nonsurvival, for Kierkegaard said, "I am ashamed, therefore I exist." At the same time Rebazar Tarzs, a Tibetan ECK Master well versed in ECKANKAR, refuted this by quoting from an ancient manuscript, the Shariyat-Ki-Sugmad, the Way of the Eternal, that "I am eternal, therefore I am free."

18

Comparative statements fly back and forth between the two philosophies. ECKANKAR's axiom is that "Life is a reality to be experienced." Descartes, one of the early advocates of the philosophy of gloom, says, "Life is a problem to be solved."

Again we quote from the book of the ancient Shariyat-Ki-Sugmad, "Modesty is the hallmark of spirituality." But Kierkegaard reported he was ashamed so he had existence.

The ancient theory of awareness points out that "Freedom is a completeness in itself for Soul to enter into the divine illumination, or suffer the effects of reality." However, Jean-Paul Sartre argues the point, for he paints the picture that freedom is a frozen and liberating emptiness.

The old prophet of gloom, Dostoevski, muttered that "If God did not exist, everything would be possible." But on the other hand ECKANKAR makes its stand that since "God does exist, all is possible. For HE is in all things at all times, and wherever man stands is holy ground because God IS."

One of the famous statements which has been often quoted by scholars, religionists and laymen who should know better is the old Descartes statement, "I think, therefore I am." According to Rebazar Tarzs, no statement in all western philosophies shows such a misconception of truth. Since the day the great French scientist sat on a cold stove and meditated on such horrible errors, we have been riding the road of philosophy downward to nowhere. It has filled the heads of students with nonsense and false premises.

Because it is concerned with mind, it is false. Mind is the perverted machinery of man. It is the wrong-doer of the human race, simply from the fact ahat it works only in a groove like a stuck phono-needle. It was because of this very basic factor that Freud was able to build a whole philosophy and psychology of nothing around it, which ended up as a so-called cure-all device called psychoanalysis. It has been proven that the latter was and is a cult which has never cured anyone, and thank goodness it is on the way out.

Mind makes only a slave of anyone who follows its

dictates. Education today is concerned only with mind in the reflecting method of teaching, which is a sort of hypnosis. All that hypnosis is said to be is working with the reflective methods of impressing the mind to obey.

Someday we will go beyond our present educational methods and work on an altogether different phase of instruction which will be a gain over our so-called modern ways. ECKANKAR says, "I live in the true awareness of myself, the real I; therefore, I am truly myself and free." What more does anyone want?

Lastly, we go back to Descartes again and a typical statement of Existentialism. Toward the end of his life, he said, "Matter is the only reality I am able to grasp." Even Pascal beat this, for he saw all things coming out of true awareness, that which made the world of matter and lifted man into a greater being.

According to the Shariyat-Ki-Sugmad, "The true reality is spirit, in any world, and he who looks upon it as giving him existence and experience is indeed a wise man."

This extension of conscious awareness is actually a matter of good survival, as Thomas Merton, the Trappist monk and writer, kept pointing out in his very good books. That is, to depend on this conscious awareness instead of the intellect is to continue the uplifting of one's self and to gain freedom.

To depend on matter and intellect is to follow the road to destruction; and such is being done today on our college campuses and throughout the world's good junior groups.

OUT-OF-THE-BODY PROJECTION
SAVED MY LIFE

The car wreck came about in such an odd manner that I hardly realized what had happened until it became apparent that my physical body was lying on the road unconscious and I was looking at it curiously.

I was driving fast up over a high rocky area in a new sports car which had been purchased in Italy a few weeks before, heading west on what is called the Gold Coast road which edges around the towering heights overlooking the blue Mediteranean.

In fact, I was driving faster than common sense said was safe on this sharp curving road. But I was too elated about having a solid little foreign sports car and was sure that it would hold to the road without too much trouble.

Suddenly I became aware that somebody was sitting in the seat beside me in the early afternoon sunlight; the man was dressed in a familiar dark red robe with a cowl like those the medieval monks wore. He had snapping black eyes and a short-cropped beard, and his hair was likewise short.

His appearance, so suddenly, did not startle me too much; he was Rebazar Tarzs, a Tibetan lama who lives in the Hindu Kush mountains in central Asia, near the great 25,000 foot peak called Tirich Mir. He often appears like this to me.

"You won't make this next curve," he said, although it wasn't a vocal message. "Get ready to jump!"

"Jump?" I cried, looking over the cliff's edge. Some hundred feet below the sea foamed angrily over the sharp, jagged rocks.

Suddenly I sprang out of the body and looked at the car. From the position of being three feet above my head, in what is known as the Atma projection, I could see that the car was heading for disaster. I could never make it.

Rebazar Tarzs signaled swiftly, "Jump!"

Springing back into the body, I flung it sidewise and went tumbling over the hard road, feeling every rock and the pound of flesh against the surface. That was all I remembered in the physical for a long time, except for the crashing of the car metal against the rail as it went over the cliff.

Suddenly I became aware of standing in the middle of the road, with the warm sunlight flaring out around me. There was hardly a scratch on my body. My mysterious companion was a few feet away leaning against a rock. His white teeth gleamed in a wide smile.

"You always forget to take a look at that curve," he said

21

through his mind. "You forgot everything I taught you!"

"There was too much pleasure in driving that high speed car," I flashed back.

Snorting, he motioned to me. I followed him down the curve a few yards further to find something that looked like an animal lying in the road. A second glance showed it was my physical body in a crooked position. The Master leaned over and touched it with a pointed forefinger.

"Well, you're not ready to leave this thing yet," he smiled.

I groaned, "But it's completely broken up. I don't want to get back into that lump of clay."

He leaned over again and straightened out the crooked limbs. "A few bumps and bruises," he commented. "That's all!"

I heard the sound of another car coming up the road; the next thing I recalled was sitting in an emergency ward of a hospital with a doctor picking rock out of my flesh. I sat up quickly.

He shrugged. "You're lucky, Monsieur," he said in English. "By any other standards you'd be dead now, or have some pretty badly broken bones. Your car is beyond repair."

It was no accident that I came out of this catastrophe like a cat on its feet without losing any of its nine lives. I knew it was only that out-of-the-body projection skill which my half-sister had taught me when a child, and which was later developed to considerable ability by Rebazar Tarzs, that had saved my life.

The latter is a remarkable individual who can appear anywhere he wishes. He is said to be some five hundred years old, and reveals himself only to those who are seeking certain truths. He is the advocate of ECKANKAR, the ancient science of Soul travel.

This has very little to do with astral projection; in fact, astral projection is only one aspect of the teachings of ECKANKAR. Once one has become acquainted with Rebazar Tarzs and has absorbed some of his ancient teachings, it is possible that he will take his chela to the spiritual city of Agam Des, which is located in the remote wilds of the

22

Himalaya mountains.

Its name means "the inaccessible place," and it is certainly that; not only is its position hidden in those wilds, but hardly anyone visits it any more than they would Shamballa or Damcar or any of the seven spiritual cities, unless the ancient brotherhood of adepts living there wish it. One goes by invitation only, and in the light body — not the astral, or mental body — but by that which we call Atma Body, or Soul alone.

These extraordinary adepts of the East are called the Eshwar-Khanewale, in Hindu language, which is the word for God-Eaters in the inner circle of the spiritual travelers.

This ancient city is the center of activity where the line of ECKANKAR has flown through to reach this Earth planet. It was brought here in the early dawn of this world from the city of Retz, capital of the planet Venus, by a spiritual traveler who goes both ways between the worlds as an agent of God. So far, few know about this ancient science of traveling between the worlds except those within this secret brotherhood of ancient adepts.

Because the inhabitants of the other planets normally have a higher intelligence than those of this planet, they are usually followers of ECKANKAR, and some are members of the same secret brotherhood of adepts. These adepts often make stops at the secret spiritual cities on Earth during their travels between the planets and constellations of this universe.

My first experience in the field of Soul travel came at the early age of three, when my older half-sister taught me the art. Most of my family were able to do spiritual traveling on their own initiative and explore the other worlds.

Years later we went to India to study under an eastern adept, Sudar Singh, in his ashram at Allahabad, and learned more about out-of-the-body travel. It was on a second trip there I discovered Rebazar Tarzs, the Tibetan adept, and went to the Himalayas to study with him a short time.

I passed through a series of teachers at Rebazar Tarzs'

request, to learn something under each, as each was a specialist in his own right, but came back to the ancient teachings of ECKANKAR. This adept, Rebazar Tarzs, is able to project himself thousands of miles over land and sea to anyone he wishes, or to any place in this universe or the spiritual worlds. He uses the Atma projection technique, or what we call Soul projection. I have given it the name of direct projection, which was the technique I used in the example of getting out of the sports car when it went over the cliff on the curve that day.

This is a skill that many people can learn, like those who have attended my ECKANKAR workshops at the Parapsychology Foundation.

ECKANKAR is the key for unlocking the secrets of the universe. It is a proof of survival of man after death, for it gives evidence that all things have life beyond this physical plane, including animals, plants and minerals.

Therefore, the purpose of ECKANKAR is simply to reach that realm of spirit which is known as the Kingdom of God. Hence, it is the modus operandi that we, as Soul, use as the vehicle to reach the heavenly realm.

The basic aspect of ECKANKAR is freedom, a liberation from the physical body. Once anyone has learned it he is free to come and go at will in spirit form. When death occurs, he can leave the physical body and enter into the spiritual worlds and be with whom he wishes.

On the road that day, when traveling at a high speed, I knew that a crash was coming because I was able to get out of the body by direct projection and see for myself. Of course the sudden appearance of Rebazar Tarzs was the cause of my taking a look; but it was possible that I might have seen for myself if he hadn't come. I have been in other tight spots and pulled out alone. But this time, going at such a high speed, and enjoying myself so thoroughly, it might have been a serious crackup if he hadn't called my attention to the impending danger.

Regardless of how much we are developing in the ability of

getting out of the body, there is always a certain amount of protection afforded us by the spiritual travelers with whom we have come in contact during our travels in the other worlds.

THE INVISIBLE
REALM OF SPIRIT

The invisible realm of Spirit is a vast world lying beyond what the human race calls the earth planet and which apparently has not been examined by either the scientists or politicians for material glory.

It is a magnificent series of spiritual universes where the Tuza (Soul) goes following the disposal of its earthly body in that phenomenon called death, and where so many persons travel in their light body from the earth plane.

The invisible realm has many names. The Greeks called it the Elysian Fields, or the Isles of the Blessed, Happy Isles, Fortunate Isles, or the Garden of Hesperides; the Scandinavians gave it the name of Valhalla and Asgard; the American Indians knew it as the Happy Hunting Grounds, and the Hebrews called it Canaan, or the Promised Land. The Buddhists all know it as Nirvana, and the Christians have named it Paradise or Heaven. Other religions have various names for this afterworld where all disembodied entities live.

Rudyard Kipling wrote a story of a boy who had a glimpse of this Far Country. Occasionally he would see the vision as he progressed into manhood. He yearned to enter that heavenly abode, but had no way except through death. When dying from a wound received in battle during World War I, he sees a vision of this invisible world and knows at last he is ready to enter. The short story is called "The Far Country."

Those who have had a glimpse of this strange realm of God are always unhappy with their existence on this earth planet. Unless they learn the art of Soul travel, these people become extremely restless. Some will commit suicide in hopes of reaching it, but this defeats their purpose.

Tom Lea, the American author, wrote a novel called "The Wonderful Country," which was a story of a range rider who restlessly searched the Southwest on his magnificent black stallion for that world which exists but is never found because few persons ever find out about ECKANKAR, or what we know as out-of-the-body projection, until after they have left the physical body permanently.

Many persons have a knowledge of the Invisible Realms of Spirit, although they are neither fortunate enough to witness it in visions nor can they travel through the esoteric planes in the light body like those who have the knowledge and ability to leave their bodies by controlled projection.

Those explorers of the other worlds — Kabir, Guru Nanak, Saint Paul, Christ, Zoroaster, Buddha, Tulsi Das, Samus-i-Tabriz and others too many to name here — have been pioneers of the Far Country. They have left a living saga which we must study and admire for their adventurous spirit.

These great ones have given us a philosophy to live by, but much of it has been misused and often employed for individual gain instead of the universal cause of mankind.

One of the bolder spirits who constantly explore the realms of God is Rebazar Tarzs, a Tibetan lama, living in the wildest region of the Himalayas near the Afghanistan and Kashmir borders where they are joined by the Hindu Kush range.

The real contribution of those like Rebazar Tarzs has been the description of these mystic lands beyond the physical worlds, and which have matched many of my own explorations.

The scientist looks at the heavens from an objective point of view and makes use of the canopy of air for the purpose of helping mankind, but the mystics start from the interior vision, or with the spiritual eye.

The scientists say there are five layers in the atmosphere, lying upward and that we are like the primitive savage standing on the shores of an ocean wondering how far the water stretches beyond the setting sun.

They call these regions or layers the troposphere,

tropopause, stratosphere, ionosphere and the unknown. The mystics call them the Astral, Brahm Lok, Daswan Dwar, Maha Sunna, Sach Khand, and beyond these are other planes called Alakh Lok. Agam Lok and Anami Lok.

The Vedantists call these planes the Astral, Mental, Wisdom, Bliss and God-plane.

The difference being the objective side of these planes are seen by the physical scientists, and the subjective by the mystics. Of course, the mystics can come and go at will in their spiritual body in and through any plane they so desire.

According to the spiritual travelers, the first plane is called the Astral, known as the Anda, the lowest of the heavens. It lies nearest to the physical world and is known to the scientist as the troposphere. The lower part of this world is the gross material or earth planet and its fellow worlds. Coarse matter dominates all but a few minds and souls.

This region embraces all the suns and planets known or unknown to astronomy. It extends out into space, a fact which is not part of the knowledge of scientists, far beyond the reach of any telescope. The mystics, or spiritual travelers, a name which I have given to those who can leave the physical body at will and travel through these invisible realms, come and go in this region to help those who live in this world.

The capital of this world is at the top of the Astral region. It is called Sahasra Dal Kanwal, which means the thousand petalled lotus, the center of the occult part of man that all yogis strive to reach for spiritual attainment.

According to the spiritual travelers, the overlord of this world, in the spiritual hierarchy of the invisible realms is Jot Niranjan. He is the center of the power commonly called the thousand petalled lotus, the great cluster of lights which is the series of illuminations that the traveler views when approaching the higher astral planes. This is the actual powerhouse of the physical universe and what the scientists have been striving to understand. They have come to the duality of the atom turning from its spiritual refinement together with the coarser side to make up matter experienced

27

by the physical scientists.

Out of this powerhouse flows the power which has created and now sustains all the worlds in the universe. These lights are of all shades and tints, but made up of the basic spectrum colors. These flow off as streams or rays through the lower universes, and each has some different aspect to help with the physical life on the planet.

The astral region is the negative pole of the whole spiritual universe. Life is so long here that many believe they have reach immortality. However, this world is often wiped out after several million years, followed by an equal period of darkness, then a new creation is started.

The second region is called the tropopause by the scientists. They think of it as being a no-man's land lying above the first region, but the travelers call it Brahmanda, which means the egg of Brahm, and referred to by the name of its overlord, Brahm. Many worship this deity as the supreme being of all creation.

This world is the second grand division, the top of the three lower worlds, the physical, lower and upper astral world.

This is the region of the spiritual-material world because spirit dominates it. This is the region of the universal mind, whose power is called AUM. Hence, it is the lower part of this region called the Home of the Universal Mind. It is from here that all individual minds are derived and return when they are discarded during the upward flight of spirit.

The Spiritual Traveler takes you on, for he alone is the guide, in your first trip through the inner worlds. He knows the path and is the recognized agent of God. All lords, rulers and peoples on every plane pay homage to him. When you arrive at the gate of this region, the sound of AUM is heard continuously like a great drum. The seeds of your karma are burned and destroyed here. The color is that of a beautiful setting sun.

Above this region is another part of the same world where you find deserts, mountains and gardens. Flowers are

28

arranged in artistic designs everywhere. You are intoxicated with joy as you wander through splendid regions of canals and streams before coming to a wide stream over which you cross by bridge to the other side where there are three mountain peaks called Mer, Sumer and Kailash.

This is the stepping off place for the spiritualists and many mystics. The yogis believe that this is their heaven. The miracles of the mind are performed from this plane, e.g., you can stop trains, fill dry wells, and heal the sick.

This world is extremely vast, despite what the scientists think, when compared with the physical universe or the astral world. There are six planes within this plane, and its chief city is on a plane called Mer Kailash.

This is the world of Brahm whose chief duty is to create, maintain and destroy the universe below it. It is the center of creation of the material and astral worlds. Many of the great scriptures have sprung from this region, including the Vedas, Christianity, and many others. Lord Krishna and many other spiritual leaders make their homes here.

The travelers call the third region Daswan Dwar. This region is filled with brilliant lights. Soul bathes itself in the lake of Mansarover, known to most of in the Old Bible as the River Jordan, where, when one is dipped in it, he is relieved of all aberrations and maya. It joins Souls, known as Hansas, who live on this plane, purified and free of all Its bodies; physical, astral, causal and mental.

Soul light here is equal to the light and radiance of a dozen physical suns together, and the happiness and bliss experienced by it at this stage is beyond words. But while here, Soul is capable of performing grand miracles, e.g., giving sight to the blind, often raising the dead, and has the ability to travel through the ether in his physical body. Here man beholds himself as pure spirit stripped of all materiality.

This is the land of the Hansas who are known on the physical plane as the Paramahansas. Very few Souls go beyond this realm, because they feel that this is the heaven that they have all searched for during their lives on Earth.

The travelers call the fourth plane the land of Sohang, through whom God power flows. He is the mystical lord of this world and lives in a city of great light called Arhirit. When Soul reaches here it is filled with majestic beauty and grandeur, and it says to itself, "I am That!" At this moment of sublime realization, you know that you are one with All, an essential part of God. This is why the Vedantists call this the Bliss Plane!

The color of the plane is blue, for it is often spoken of as the House of Truth, and that world of true miracles from which all things can happen. But woe to him who misuses this power.

After crossing a zone of deep, dense darkness, one comes to another world, the fifth plane called the Sach Khand. Here dwells the Sat Nam, or true name, the first manifestation of God in the worlds below the Supreme regions. His brilliance is so great that one hair on his body would radiate a light equal to that of a million suns combined.

This is the true home of Soul. It is the grand headquarters of all creation and the region of immortality. It is changeless, perfect and deathless. It is called the God world by the Hindus. It is untouched by dissolution or reconstruction, a world of the saints and where they live.

The fifth region is the starting place where the Soul can rise upward into the great worlds of pure spirit. The citizens are pure spirit, in such countless numbers that no man could estimate, and there is a joy so wondrous that we on this earth plane cannot conceive of it.

When Soul comes to face the Lord of this region, It says, "I am He!" Once he becomes self-realized, Soul understands that Love is the only bond that holds all the worlds together. Only the spiritual travelers can reach this region and travel into the next worlds above.

All the divine power flowing from the upper regions come into a perfect manifestation for the first time in the Lord of this world. He is the actual complete personification of the Supreme One, and so fathomless and impersonal we cannot approach Him even m thought. He sits between the infinite light and the created universes, and so in time, when purged of every imperfection, we approach Him as the Father and receive a gracious welcome.

Beyond this plane is the Alakh Lok plane, and then the Agam Lok. Finally after a succession of many planes, Soul reaches the end of its journey, the region of the nameless One, or the SUGMAD, the supreme lord of all that exists.

No words can describe IT and no thought can embrace IT. IT is formless, all embracing. IT is the impersonal, infinite ocean of love. From IT flows all life and spirituality, all truth, all reality. IT is all wisdom and love and power. All visible lords of the regions below are ITS manifestations. IT takes forms, many forms, in order that ITS purpose might be carried out in all creations. They are all ITS forms; none of them express ITS totality. IT may take millions of shapes, but IT ITSELF remains formless, impersonal, all pervading. IT is universal spirit, universal life.

When Soul reaches here it is so absorbed in its joy, lost in its splendor, that It at once realizes the futility of even attempting to explain.

ECKANKAR
THE SCIENCE OF SOUL TRAVEL

When I first encountered Rebazar Tarzs, one of the world's greatest adepts, the torchbearer for ECKANKAR, ancient science of Soul travel, in the hill country north of Darjeeling, my life made a drastic change.

I had already had a lifetime of out-of-the-body experiences, but he had something which was my destiny to have as a part of the divine knowledge, ECKANKAR, which has now become as much of myself as eating and sleeping. I had grown up in a family which could do exteriorization very well, especially a half-sister who had taught me at the age of three how to get out of the body at will.

But at this particular time I was hiking through the high

31

hills of Upper Bengal, along a trail which would lead up to a 12,000 foot pass into Sikkim and eventually to Tibet, that mysterious land of the lamas. My sole purpose was to find the elusive Tibetan lama, known as Rebazar Tarzs, of whom I had heard much from the late Sudar Singh at Allahabad. This lama, Rebazar Tarzs, was one of those who had escaped the Chinese who had invaded his country, and it was said that he now lived in the hill country close by.

Stories about this wondrous saint who was the advocate of ECKANKAR fired my imagination. ECKANKAR is the ancient art of traveling in the jiva body anywhere one wishes.

It was a hot summer afternoon in 1951. I was worn out with my search and about to return to the hotel in Darjeeling. There had been no signs of him unless he had disguised himself as one of the ragged natives who could hardly speak but a handful of English words.

It was a lonely hike, with the deep silence of the forests and emptiness of space. I dared not to leave the beaten path to enter one of the many white-capped monasteries dotting the hills. The natives in the villages were friendly but would become silent when I asked about Rebazar Tarzs. Some would nod, grin and divert the talk to the Yeti, but now and then drop a hint about that strange brotherhood of ancient adepts called the Eshwar-Khanewale, whom I came later to know as the God-eaters.

Sudar Singh often spoke of Rebazar Tarzs, a Tibetan saint, whom he said was reputed to be over five hundred years old, and was at the time living in the foothills between Darjeeling and Gangtock somewhere, but presently has a small abode in the Hindu Kush mountains on the Afghanistan-Kashmir frontier, near Tibet.

This great adept is in the same line of masters descending from Rama, one of the first known world teachers who had the unique ability to travel in the Tuza (Soul) form, and was the original teacher of the secret science known as ECKANKAR. Rebazar Tarzs is the present messenger of the holy science of Soul travel.

I reached an open glade about two in the afternoon and seated myself to eat a small lunch, wondering if it would ever be possible to meet with this unique wondermaker, vaguely hoping it would come about in some manner or other.

Nothing happened. There were no sounds except the wind stirring the overhead boughs. Then, suddenly, there he was — a man in a dark maroon robe, about knee length — standing only a few yards away and looking at me with eyes that gleamed like coals of shining fire.

He was about five feet ten and had a black cropped beard and hair. His feet were bare and his square hands lightly held a small staff in front of himself.

Jumping up, I stared at him.

"Don't be frightened." He spoke good English in a clipped speech. "No harm will come to you."

"Who are you?" I asked in surprise.

"I am Rebazar Tarzs," he smiled, gesturing with the forefinger of his left hand. "Don't ask that question. You will learn soon enough how I knew you were looking for me."

He seated himself in the lotus posture in the heavy grass. "I've been watching you while I was in the Atma Sarup."

It meant that he was in the Soul form watching me hike around the foothills in search of him. "I've been looking for you to ask you about ECKANKAR."

I described my stay at Allahabad, and the many things told me about the mysterious but secret science of ECKANKAR in connection with his name.

He smiled. "Why do you wish to gain the knowledge of this God science?"

"To learn truth. Mainly the path of ECKANKAR may lead me to God; others have failed. I know that you teach it as it originally came to this planet many centuries ago by oral teachings."

He closed his eyes and sat in silence for what seemed eternity. This strange adept who was at the time living in an icy cave in the Himalayas often leaves his physical body and goes out into the universe, or those beyond this physical plane, to those aware of ECKANKAR, or teaches in a wisdom temple or some planet, or in the invisible planes, to teach ECKANKAR, the ancient science of controlled Soul travel.

Frequently he appears in Agam Des, the spiritual city of the ancient brotherhood, the Eshwar-Khanewale, or God-Eaters, which is located near the high peak of Tirich Mir in central Asia. Here he holds what we would call a teaching chair at the famous ECK-Marg School of Wisdom.

This city is one of the great spiritual cities here on this earth planet. Among these is the legendary Shamballa in India. There are similar spiritual cities located on the major planets in this universe.

The God-Eaters are so named because they consume cosmic energy instead of material food, as humans do. This is their official domicilary on this planet. They move between the planets, the invisible planes, and among the people on Earth. Sometimes they are called spiritual travelers, those that have the ability to move by the Atma Sarup at anytime and anywhere.

ECKANKAR is the ancient science of Soul travel taught only by the higher adepts to those who have advanced spiritually to the point to be trusted in leaving the physical body temporarily while Soul explores the worlds of this universe, including the planets and constellations, or the invisible worlds where we go after death of the physical body.

Leaving the body in the Atma Sarup is different from astral projection, which is well known in the annals of religion and occult sciences. Often called Soul travel, this form of motion via Soul differs mainly from the astral travel by the fact that we use the state of consciousness instead of any of the other subtle bodies, i.e., the astral, causal and mental bodies.

Most of those who are interrested in the esoteric science are aware of astral traveling. The astral body is an exact duplicate of the physical body we wear, except it is of a much finer vibratory form, and is connected with the imaginative faculty and emotions. The consciousness is that state in which we have an ability to look, know and be. When we travel beyond the Soul plane, known as the fifth plane of God, into the higher realms of spirit, we will gain freedom, charity and wisdom. We can go anywhere we wish and do anything within the spiritual and material worlds that is within reason and authority of God. At least we are free of the lower world phenomenon.

The astral plane is, of course, a limited region. It is mainly concerned with the lower aspects of life, e.g., ESP, telepathy, levitation, astral traveling and psychic powers. On the other hand, Atma Sarup traveling leads to illumination, cosmic consciousness and eventually to becoming a co-worker with God.

It gives us freedom to be anywhere we wish in the higher or lower planes, on any planet, or in this world of the earth, in any form invisible to others. It gives us a choice to help, or not, with people who are wanting spiritual assistance. But we do this under our own volition; in other words, we can come and go at our own will.

This ancient art came to this planet via Venus, in the dawn of time here. Rama, the legendary saviour who took this art to India, even before the Aryan invasion, taught it secretly and orally. It came down in this manner through the centuries as a secret teaching until Kabir, the Hindu mystic, began teaching it openly. Many medieval saints, like St. Anthony of Padua, were proficient at this art. Padre Pio at the San Giovanni Rotondo monastery in Italy is said to be one also to practice Soul travel at will.

Since this first meeting with Rebazar Tarzs it has been proved many times over, especially when he appeared nightly for a period to dictate a full manuscript called "The Far Country", a whole discourse on ECKANKAR, in my apartment in San Francisco while his body was lying on a crude bed in a hut high in the Hindu Kush mountains.

When he had finished his first discourse on ECKANKAR

35

on that hot afternoon in the hills of ancient India, he rose and smiled. "It is getting late. I will walk with you to the suburbs of the city. Come!"

We went down the trail silently to the edge of the city where he paused. My mind was in such a whirl that I wondered if this was a dream. "It is not a dream," he said, answering my question, "but a reality." Men always want to be given signs and wonders. Jesus was bothered with this hindrance in His time.

"Look," he said, touching my arm. "I'm solid flesh. Can you understand this in your confused state?"

I nodded.

He stepped to the side of the trail and pushed back the thick brush. To my utter surprise, there lying beneath the foliage was an exact duplicate of himself looking for all the world as if in serene slumber.

Smiling, he snapped his fingers. The body on the ground stirred, sat up and opened its eyes. Shocked, I turned to speak, but that form which had sat, walked and talked with me, had disappeared. One moment he was standing there and next gone.

"Don't be surprised," he said, standing up and brushing off his robe. "It's nothing more than manifesting bodies when needed."

He put out his hand and shook mine in western style. "We will be meeting often."

That was all, and the path was empty again.

He has kept his word, coming and going when he wills it, giving out the ancient science of ECKANKAR when necessary. I have found it to be a useful, reliable skill which can be used at any level of life.

THE STRANGE CITY OF
THE ANCIENT BROTHERHOOD

The spiritual city of Agam Des is near the tremendous peak of Tirich Mir, which is some 25,000 feet in height in

36

central Asia on the border of Kashmir and Afghanistan.

Its name means the inaccessible world and it certainly is. Not only is its position hidden deep in these remote wilds, but few shall visit the place, any more than they would visit Shamballa unless the ancient brotherhood of God-Eaters wishes. One goes by invitation only, and then by the Nuri Sarup which is the light body of the individual — the self within.

This strange city is known only to a few adepts who are called the Eshwar-Khanewale, or what we know in English as the God-Eaters, by the inner circle of the spiritual travelers.

When I first heard of this mysterious group of adepts and their incredible teachings, it was impossible to believe. They are said to be controlling the secret forces of the cosmic life which gives human history its many changes and shapes in this world.

It was only after I made contact with the spiritual traveler known as Rebazar Tarzs, the great Tibetan lama who is reputed to be over 500 years old, via the Atma Sarup, separation of spirit from the body at will, that I became acquainted with the ancient brotherhood of the God-Eaters in their secret city of Agam Des.

Rebazar Tarzs brought to my attention the mysterious facet of philosophy known as the ancient art of ECKANKAR — the science of Soul travel.

ECKANKAR is the philosophy of the phardar pax latehue walae, or what we know as the Cliffhangers, the sociological hero of the present times. My development of it in the latter phase for modern life in opposition to Existentialism, which has become the materialistic philosophy that engulfs youth today, grew out of my visits to Agam Des, the city of the God-Eaters. The basic axiom of this philosophy is: Man is a spiritual co-worker of God, and has access to freedom, charity and wisdom. He always exists through eternity as the ECK.

It is through the supernatural energy that the God-Eaters can supervise the spiritual law. However, they have this ability because the supernatural energy is only secondary to the knowledge of the spiritual law.

37

These extraordinary adepts of the Far East are actually God-Eaters, not in the symbolic sense that the Christians eat the body of Christ in the sacramental cracker and drink the Saviour's blood as the wine, but they eat the cosmic energy which is God. They do this purposely for survival as the homo sapiens eats material foods to keep his body alive.

Until one learns to live outside the physical body in the spiritual self no progress can be expected in the spiritual life of any individual. Only then will he be able to give up the foods of the earth world and live as the God-Eaters who consume the cosmic spirit as their food. I found evidence of this truth in the "Autobiography of a Yogi" by Paramahansa Yogananda. He tells of a woman he knew who had no physical food for thirty years. St. Catherine of Sienna was another who was an eater of the cosmic spirit. There are numerous examples of those who are consumers of the cosmic spirit in religious history.

These God-Eaters absorb the cosmic energy at a fantastic rate. By doing so they use their physical bodies in the universe to serve the races of the many planets, including the earth world. They serve, not merely because the spiritual law demands service, but in interest to themselves, for should the atmosphere become too loaded with radiation, they would have to move to another planet or universe. They work best from the earth because the flow of cosmic particles is greater than in other parts of the universe.

This fantastic assemblage of spiritual beings do their work under a supernatural leader named Yaubl Sacabi. I was received by this exalted being through Rebazar Tarzs. He accompanied me to this strange city which looked something like the land of Oz. Baird Spalding touched upon the truth in his book, "The Life and Teaching of the Masters of the Far East," but never got close to Agam Des. He was kept away for reasons unknown.

The God-Eaters are said to have a longevity like the spiritual beings in Spalding's books, which would put the aged citizens of Hunza down as babes-in-arms. It is reputed they revitalized their bodies when necessary with the cosmic spirit. Yaubl Sacabi is said to be an ancient being in age, yet when I have seen him while visiting Agam Des he appeared to be a man in his middle thirties.

Some occult groups come nearer the truth than they realize. The Cabalists named their hierarchy in an order which closely resembles the God-Eaters' arrangement of spiritual government. Madame Blavatsky was inside this spiritual city Agam Des years ago and she named these beings the White Brotherhood for reasons of her own. The early Sufis knew something of the truth of these secret teachers. Plato called them the shadowy people Frater X writes of a similar group in South America called the Green Robe Monks.

Agam Des is one of the seven spiritual cities on this globe. Another, Shamballa, is located in India, two others in South America, one each in Guatamala, Spain and Africa. Brown Landone has given treatment to the spiritual cities of South America in his books.

The God-Eaters insist on one law being obeyed, that which concerns the welfare of themselves. "Speak not, nor harm not those who eat of the flesh of God. For harm comes to him who does!"

George Fox, founder of Quakerism, is the best example to portray what happens to those who bring harm to a godly Soul. Read his journals for such data. Anyone who has eaten of the flesh of God is immune to harm in any manner. I know this from personal experience.

THE ANCIENT CREED
OF ECKANKAR

The ancient creed of ECKANKAR was first brought to my attention by Rebazar Tarzs, and further expounded upon by that inner circle of highly spiritual travelers known as the God-Eaters who live in the spiritual city of Agam Des.

The ancient creed within itself is adequate to lead any neophyte to his ultimate aim which is the knowledge of the true self, the Tuza, or Soul, as it is known in the language of the upper planes, and eventually to that deity called the SUGMAD, or God, by the followers of ECKANKAR.

All religious groups have creeds which are definite routes to lead the seeker toward a specific place, but few take the spiritual aspirant to hardly more than the astral plane. The makers of creeds generally know truth, but they also know the limited conditions of humanity as a whole.

However, the God-Eaters, in preparing the way for the human race, set forth the ancient creed many years ago. All other creeds are practically in the infant stages when compared with that of the ancient creed of SUGMAD.

Those creeds established by the orthodox religions are not exactly perfect. We have many, e.g., the Apostles, Nicene, and the Athanasian creeds, to name a few. These are each an authoritative formula of religious belief, or what might be called a summary of principles or opinions, professed or adhered to in religion, science or politics.

The spiritual travelers, those individuals who can come and go between the physical worlds and the spiritual universes, are the support and the foundation of the ancient creed of ECKANKAR. Rebazar Tarzs, a highly developed spiritual traveler of Tibet, pointed out to me that perfection cannot be reached through the creeds of religion because they are limited.

"Perfection has no limitation nor is it temporary or changeable, while pleasure and suffering are conditions of material existence," Rebazar Tarzs said.

The ancient creed of ECKANKAR is, therefore, that "All life flows from SUGMAD, downward into the worlds below, and through them, and nothing can exist without this cosmic current known as Shabda, which can be heard as sound and seen as light. Therefore, it is necessary for man always to be aware of the sounds of ECK and see the Nuri of the SUGMAD in order to live within the highest spiritual realms."

This is the true belief of the spiritual travelers who have

40

visited the higher realms and traveled the path of ECK-Marg. The secret knowledge is not something to read from a book. It is a process through which the neophyte slowly develops and prepares himself. He does not acquire the sound and light of the SUGMAD; he becomes a part of it. He does not accept it, for it accepts him.

As one studies and practices to reach the higher worlds, he gradually comes to the realization that all life is sound and light, flowing out of the Godhead somewhere within himself. As he grows more aware of it, he comes into God-Realization and knows that the source of this sound and light which is within himself is only a part of that universal sound and light flowing from above.

When he realizes this, and accepts the SUGMAD as that source, his life will become greater in every aspect.

BE TWO PLACES
AT THE SAME TIME

Today we have a strange paradox existing in our world, especially in America where the basic concept of political government is to give its citizens more security than ever has been known in the history of any nation previous to these times.

We have security in so many various ways, yet people are turning to the path of God despite the fact that more comforts are given to the body, pleasures for the mind, and succor for the Soul in such quantities that it sometimes overwhelms the individual.

It is this search for even greater security that eventually turns one inwardly to seek the spiritual kingdom. Usually it is not the desire for perfection that starts the seeking, but the Soul seeking its own in the world of Spirit from which it came originally.

Soul travel can be the way and means of understanding how anyone may find the procedures of reaching security. Soul travel is exactly what the name implies, being in two places or more at the same time. It is a study of the separation of the Spirit from the body, also known by various other names, such as — exteriorization, projection, out-of-the-body experiences, and spiritual traveling, to name a few. Some are able to project consciously at will, while others find themselves at varied times out of the body without having consciously willed it.

ECKANKAR is the main key for unlocking the secrets of the spiritual universe, although for many it does not give the same degree of satisfaction and confidence in seeking out the hidden mysteries of the Spirit. Much of the problem, however, lies in semantics, or the language used to describe it. Those who can travel into the far worlds beyond this plane are not able to give us an accounting of their experiences for the reason that spiritual semantics have not yet been developed to the point that we can understand what they are saying. It is like the Buddhist monks who speak to one another by signs because words are inadequate to describe their experiences of the wonders of God they beheld while outside of the body.

Man's development in consciousness since ancient days had been somewhat slowed up until the birth of Christ, then the pace quickened until the Renaissance, and after that the consciousness of man unfolded quickly. The nineteenth century saw the development of so many things for our higher consciousness that we have become dizzy with inventions and creations from our mental realm.

After a long study of spiritual wisdoms, I came up with the conclusion that the cardinal metaphysical systems could be placed in three simple, basic classifications: the Intellectual or Mind theory, the Cosmic Consciousness theory, and the Bilocation theory. The Intellectual or Mind Theory is that which is built upon the principle that all is Mind, that the divine source of Mind is God, that all begins here and ends here, and that we must be prepared to receive all here and now, instead of having to wait for a life in the hereafter. The Chou dynasty of China was responsible for Mind

42

development a few hundred years before Christ. A mentalism was brought into maturity, then religion and several other faiths in the Orient, and far in advance of later western thinkers. The Cosmic Consciousness theory is that which is the basis of Hinduism which makes up the warp and fiber of East Indian life. The Hindu's religious mind is deep and complicated; he sees every problem as the whole and work from the whole into its parts so he can understand better that with which he is faced. The Vedas, source of the sacred scriptures for the Cosmic Consciousness theory, are the first known records of religious writing, estimated to be at least ten thousand years old. Cosmic Consciousness is known to the westerner more simply as union with God, or Oneness. It gives one the realization that we live in a brotherhood with all peoples and all things here and beyond, and that God is with us everywhere. The Bilocation theory, also known under some of the names previously mentioned, has had quite a drubbing from the followers of the Mind theory and modern psychology, and those who are disciples of the Cosmic Consciousness theory have not received it with open arms. Despite these differences, the growth in the field of Soul travel has been rapid. Soul travel should not have any particular reason for being affiliated with the astral plane only, as many spiritual students are led to believe. It is actually a way of being able to travel freely through all spiritual planes up to the Ultimate or to what we call God; certainly not to be localized in one particular plane for the sake of itself.

Those who are able to leave their bodies at will and travel through the heavenly worlds are called spiritual travelers. They are the explorers of those vast spiritual continents, far beyond the astral world, who have brought back records of what is beyond this physical plane which man will find when he passes beyond the veil of death.

The Soul traveler system was initiated, or was first known in our records of spiritual travels, by Zoroaster, the Persian avatar, some few hundred years before the coming of Christ.

There are scattered records of Soul travel experiences that go back for many centuries prior to the Persian mystics; however, they are lost in the dim, misty past, and we cannot separate legend from truth in some reports. Most of the teachings of the magian mystics developed out of tenets laid down by this Persian (Iranian) sage. They were the original magi, ancestors of the Sufi mystics, and it was from among these magi groups that the messengers came who went to see Jesus at the time of his birth. We know them as "The Three Wise Men from the East." The basic principle in Soul travel is that man can take control of spiritual body and move from the visible planes to the invisible. He can help the Soul of any person who has crossed the borders of what we call physical death and put them into the hands of friends. He also can instruct and guide others to the higher planes. The three basic aspects of Soul travel are: wisdom, charity and freedom. Those who have become spiritual travelers are able to have individualized freedom, coupled with wisdom and charity, the Christian word for love, although here it is more aptly an expression for unattached good will for all. The spiritual traveler demonstrates that those who leave their body and return at will become co-workers with God, rather than join in union with Him. The Christian faith is founded more upon the Soul travel principle than that of Cosmic Consciousness for it was Christ who proved that in the spirit form, man is free. Although many saints in the Christian church have been seekers of the Cosmic Consciousness, or what is known as the enlightened mind. Most of them, as the records prove, were followers of the principle of Soul travel. The individualization of the human consciousness is freedom. Where we find security and union in Cosmic Consciousness, we find individualization and freedom in ECKANKAR. What could be more free than being able to leave your body and travel to another plane, by choice, in those far heavens to study under some great spiritual master who left this or higher planes centuries ago? Bilocation can give you this freedom. If one has a spiritual traveler or a guide to take him

44

on journeys into the other worlds, he is better equipped than trying to go it alone. Going alone may bring mistakes and suffering. You learn alright, just as in this life, but self-education is not easy until you get past the trial-and-error period.

The methods of getting out of the body are varied, some so widely it makes us wonder if we understand rightly when hearing about them. Among some of them are the antics of whirling dervishes, the sleep and dream method, and the direct projection and meditative technique.

To study the lives of the saints in the various religious organizations of the world, past and present, will give one some idea of the number of successful techniques used to develop the ability to leave the body and explore the vast worlds beyond this earth plane. You may find also, as I did, that many writers, painters, and others in the arts practice this art. Jack London, L. Adam Beck, Harriet Beecher Stowe, Elizabeth Barrett Browning, Lord Byron, Shelley, Marie Corelli, George Du Maurier and Balzac are among those too numerous to mention.

Being two places at one time is nothing new. It is just a question as to when the individual Soul is READY to choose how fast it will travel in its eternal spiritual progress.

SPACE TRAVEL BY
OUT-OF-THE-BODY PROJECTION

Space people have been coming to this planet for several thousand years for the purpose of exploration to find certain minerals and vegetation that are not in abundance on their own respective planets.

They have particular places on this planet where they land their ships safely, or use when they have arrived by direct projection from their own material bodies left on other planets to reach this world. Sometimes they have landed at the spiritual city of Agam Des, near Tirich Mir, one of the highest mountain peaks in the world. It is located in the

Hindu Kush range, part of the western Himalayas, in central Asia. It is some some 25,000 feet in height.

Other times they land in Shamballa, or Damcar, or one of the other spiritual cities on this planet. But mainly it has been Agam Des, the mysterious city of the ancient brotherhood, because of the protection it affords them from human curiosity, and because of the protection it also gives them when changing from one type of body to another. In other words, moving from the outer spaces to this lower world of coarser vibrations creates problems for those working in the much finer bodies.

Most of us who have any degree of experience in getting in and out of the body at will, in what we know as Soul travel, know of these space travelers and their landing stations on Earth. We know travelers arrive here via Soul travel from other planets, for like ourselves, they too have learned the methods of ECKANKAR, the ancient science of Soul travel.

Likewise, anyone here who has gained experience of being out of the body through this most ancient science, ECKANKAR, knows that he has the same opportunity as the space visitors to come and go as he wishes to Agam Des, or enter the city of Retz on Venus where that planet's government is established, or he can move among other planets and also through the spiritual planes to the Supreme Realm of God.

It makes little difference to anyone who has developed his latent skills in ECKANKAR for he is able to explore worlds unknown to scientists and astronauts.

Some persons who have learned these techniques of ECKANKAR, as in workshops I used to hold weekly at the Parapsychology Foundation, are able to visit other planets at will and communicate with the inhabitants there. They learn about the conditions in these worlds, but it is seldom that any of them will do much talking because the finger of derision is generally lifted at anyone who claims out-of-the-body experiences.

Rebazar Tarzs, the great Tibetan lama, reputed to be over

46

five hundred years old, was responsible for the first trips I took to the mysterious city of Agam Des. Few go to this strange place, for they must visit by invitation only, and then by the spirit body.

He brought my attention to a mysterious facet of ECKANKAR. An unknown race still living at Agam Des are known as the Eshwar-Khanewale, or simply the God-Eaters.

They are the ancient brotherhood of adepts which brought the science of ECKANKAR from Venus here thousands of years ago and have since been receiving space visitors as a way station between planets to help them make the adjustment between the worlds.

These God-Eaters attained their name because they absorb the cosmic energies instead of food as the earth people do in assimilating plants and meats. They have an extreme longevity like the patriarchs of the Old Bible, and in some cases, even longer. Many of their visitors who come to this planet via Agam Des are also known for their long life because they have learned the same trick of absorbing the cosmic energies like their brothers in the ancient circle of adepts.

These space visitors are generally members of the same order known to most of us as the Bourchakoun or the Eagle-Eyed Adepts. They are also known in India as the Vairagis, the Mystic Adepts of the Himalayas. An example is Rebazar Tarzs, who has shining coal black eyes that see like X-rays, penetrating anyone he gazes upon. Their Bible is called the Shariyat-Ki-Sugmad, or the Way of the Eternal.

Many of those in the flying saucers and those who are able to project themselves directly to this earth planet come first to Agam Des in order to acquaint themselves with the standard coarser vibrations, like those which exist in this planet.

These visitors and the inhabitants of Agam Des where they stop briefly communicate in an unknown language which is so old that it can be believed to be one of the first ever spoken on this planet.

47

THE STRANGE ADEPT
FROM TIBET

Rebazar Tarzs is one of the world's great adepts, although it is doubtful that his name is familiar to anyone who has not yet come in contact with ECKANKAR, the ancient science of Soul travel. He is the torch-bearer for ECKANKAR on the earth planet.

Rebazar Tarzs is a Tibetan lama who is said to be living in a physical body which is some five hundred years old, according to the standards we use in judging age in our physical world. He looks to be a man in his middle thirties. He is approximately six feet in height, covers his muscular 185 pounds with a maroon colored robe. He walks with a springy, youthful stride with head back and generally carries a five-foot wooden staff.

Rebazar Tarzs' black hair is cropped closely and is curly enough not to be unruly in the fierce icy mountain winds. His beard is coal black and trimmed close. His eyes are shining coals of dark fire, his lips purple and his speech a clipped style as he barks words to emphasize points he makes. His flesh is dark, swarthy from the hot sun and winds.

His restless hands are square with long, blunt fingers. He uses the forefinger of his left hand frequently to make a point. His feet are big, generally encased in sandals, but often he goes barefooted among the rocks and sand.

Rebazar Tarzs lives alone in a little mud-brick hut high on a cliff above the roaring Swat River. Miles across the valley lie the wild outposts of Afghanistan, and beyond are the jagged peaks of the Hindu Kush mountains.

His crude hut is a way station between the earth planet and the other worlds where the Tuza (Soul in ECKANKAR language) can find its guide to make a cross-over into the life beyond.

Often leaving his physical body on the crude bed inside his hut, Rebazar Tarzs goes out in his Nuri Sarup (the light body) to the Tuza who needs his help, or to teach in a temple on some other planet or in the visible worlds, or to teach the ancient science of ECKANKAR to others who have unfolded to this point.

ECKANKAR is the ancient teaching of out-of-the-body experience which is taught only by the high adepts to a number who have advanced spiritually enough to be trusted to leaving their bodies behind and exploring the worlds of this universe or beyond the invisible veils normally where the Tuza goes after death of the physical body.

Sudar Singh was the only living adept whom I knew to be teaching this ancient science of Soul travel openly. At his ashram in Allahabad he often gave the initiation to neophytes who wanted to learn this art. I have talked with and taken down the words of Sudar Singh who appeared in my apartment in Washington, D.C. in his light body, although his physical body was six thousand miles away in India.

Shabda Yoga, one of the little yogas in India, likely grew out of ECKANKAR during the l6th century when Kabir, the Hindu poet-weaver, began to teach it to a large number of followers. The old Sufi groups in Persia were adept at leaving their bodies and traveling through the other worlds, as well as this one. Jalal din'l Rumi and many of his contemporaries in the 8th century in Persia were quite adept at this science.

Many of the medieval saints were quite proficient in the art. St. Anthony of Padua was reported to have been seen in two places at the same time, and other stories are told about the great saints being seen in distant areas while their bodies remained in a place observed by their fellow monks. Christ used this technique following his burial after the crucifixion.

ECKANKAR as taught by Rebazar Tarzs is supposedly from the direct, ancient source. It is a study of the Soul experience. Man needs to learn to leave his body at will and dwell in his spirit body on other planes. He must some day leave this fleshly temple, so he should learn that by going in and out of his body in the spirit form he can give it up to death without fear and suffering.

Soul or Tuza has three places it can dwell. It can be inside the skull, three feet behind the head, or stuck in the body. Often it can be miles away and still direct the body. If it is anywhere in the body, or encased in the skull, it is trapped and cannot leave whether the individual's consciousness desires it or not.

This Tuza is the individual consciousness, that part of man which is the true awareness of the divine power within himself. If a person's attention is inside the body, or outdrawn somewhere, he cannot successfully withdraw from his physical body.

Most of those striving for spiritual perfection lose their way and become trapped, thus failing the purpose of their creation as an individual.

If one has a guide or an adept who can take him into the other worlds or to the other planets by a period of training, he is much better than trying it alone. Going alone will bring about many mistakes and much suffering, although he learns like in this physical life, that self-education is a series of trials and errors which is not easy.

I began my study of ECKANKAR under the tutelage of Sat Guru Sudar Singh in Allahabad, India. Later I studied under Rebazar Tarzs. Both were adepts in teaching ECKANKAR, the art of the Total Awareness. I had to learn to leave my body at will and return without effort.

Most of my philosophy is expounded in my works "The Tiger's Fang," written in 1957, an expose of travel through the planes of other worlds, and "The Flute of God," written in 1959.

Also among my writings are numerous casebooks containing discourses from many masters in the flesh and those on the inner planes, including visits to Agam Des, one of the spiritual cities similar to the legendary city of Shamballa, high in the remote Himalayas where dwell the strange adepts who are called Eshwar-Khanewale, or what are known to the inner circle of occultists as the God-Eaters.

In the study of the lives of the saints of all religions, I found that those who followed the philosophical principles of ECKANKAR, whether they were aware or not of doing so, were closer to the SUGMAD (God) than those who strive along the paths of other teachings.

OUT-OF-THE-BODY PROJECTION TWICE SAVED ME!

The ability to project myself from the physical body has saved my life a couple of times when in extreme danger.

Several years ago, while traveling through the Cascade Mountains in western Washington on a long trip home, I was fatigued and impatient to finish the journey. While traveling behind a slow moving truck up a high pass, I decided to move around it and started pulling over the yellow line. Second thoughts caused me to wonder if this was the right thing to do for another car might be speeding down that long, treacherous curve. So I projected myself out of the body and looked ahead to see if it was safe to continue passing around the truck. But I saw another car filled with teenagers careening down the road at high speed. I was able to pull back behind the truck in time to prevent a head-on crash.

During World War II, while ashore for a few hours on the Island of Saipan, when my ship was in port for several days, I decided to take a stroll in the wooded hills to get my land legs again. But the sentries warned me that Japanese brigands still roamed the outbrush despite the occupation by our armed forces.

But I was a disbeliever and if it hadn't been for my ability to do ECKANKAR, the separation of spirit from the physical body at will on a moment's notice, I might have lost my life.

While walking up a woodsy trail on this particular short excursion into the hills, I suddenly felt the presence of danger. My knowledge of ECKANKAR instantly came into play by direct projection from the body and viewing the landscape from approximately fifteen feet above my head.

What I saw was a frightening scene. Two armed men, apparently Japanese, judging from their physical

51

characteristics, were lying in ambush several yards up the trail waiting for me. I fled back to safety in a sprint that broke the world's record for the hundred yard dash.

Soul travel is a specialized spiritual phenomenon. I learned it from an older half-sister when a child. Everybody in my family was able to do it to some degree. Later I studied under Sudar Singh in Allahabad, India who was quite proficient at this phenomenon.

Following this, I found Rebazar Tarzs, the great Tibetan lama who was teaching ECKANKAR, the ancient art of controlled projection. Although I met with him near Darjeeling, he has lived in the Hindu Kush mountains on the western border of the Kashmir.

This lama is fantastic, and though he seems to be in his middle thirties, it is said that he is several hundred years old. Whether there is any truth in the story, I have no way of proving, but he is a master of bilocation and can easily appear in two places at the same time regardless of distance.

I have used ECKANKAR throughout my life, e.g., while hunting gold in New Guinea and was successful in getting my share, diving for pearls in South America, in penetrating the dark mysteries of voodoo ritual in the West Indies, while attempting to scale an Alaskan mountain peak on a dare, and once when the car brakes failed and I almost went over a steep cliff.

It has served me during my newspaper career, while serving as a Navy officer during World War II, as a public relations counsel, and in my present career as an author.

Its help is tremendous for I write several hours daily, skip read several thousand books a year, sleep hardly more than four hours a night, and maintain a heavy lecture schedule. Besides this, I work with hundreds of people a year who are interested in learning about ECKANKAR. Most of them catch the knack of leaving their bodies at will in a few short sessions.

After many years of studying bilocation in far-off places in this world, I took the teachings of ECKANKAR, and what I had learned from many mystic groups, and codified them into five simple techniques for getting out of the body under my own control. Now I believe that I can teach ECKANKAR to anybody.

Most people can do Soul travel easily for it is as normal as eating and sleeping. I have taught dozens of persons to do it successfully under their own control. Some in a single session and others who take a little longer.

Its philosophy is that we have proof of survival after death. Something that many people do not believe, especially the Existentialist crowd. ECKANKAR has been making inroads among the followers of Existentialism, especially in Europe among the intellectuals and college circles, after the publishing of some of my works in European journals there.

The true purpose of ECKANKAR is actually that it is another path to God, and many are following it. In the ancient days it was handed down by oral instructions. Most of my teachings of it are by the same method, although some get it in another manner.

I know of no other person today in the Occidental countries teaching ECKANKAR and practically none in the East, other than Rebazar Tarzs, the Tibetan Yogi.

A VIOLATION
OF THE LAW

Any means of trying to change anyone's mind or influence him, including prayer, without permission, is a violation of the law of God.

It is as criminal to use any occult technique upon another's consciousness as it is to rob or kill in this material world. But prayer is often used by those skillful in this specialized form of moving the spirit to manifest goals and means in the outer.

Prayer in the hands of a ruthless man or anyone with great authority will bring results readily, but always the user must pay the penalty. Church history speaks of many saints who moved the consciousness of criminals as they mounted the steps of the scaffold and of a last minute conversion. Religious history of the western church is filled with such anecdotes in praise of the saintly power, but it is a violation to move another person for any purpose whatsoever without permission.

More harm is done in prayer for another to change his consciousness than any other form of occult technique. But it is one of the common practices of the clergy to change the consciousness of the nonconformist so he cannot harm the cause of the church.

Every man has his right to freedom without interference from another. He must be granted psychic space or what is called beingness. When anyone interferes with this freedom of another, crowds his space, nature will exact a severe penalty.

Nobody has the power to judge what is good for another person's consciousness. This is the individual's own superior right in the Kingdom of God. Everyone must have his own freedom of will and thought and the opportunity to exercise this freedom.

All mass media today is guilty of flagrantly disobeying this law of God. Newspapers, TV, radio, magazines and books are produced steadily to influence readers to think and move in certain prescribed channels.

But what is the difference between praying for one to change consciousness and a newspaper publisher trying to change the readers of his publication through editorials that are slanted for certain purposes in social or political arenas? Even advertising is a form of practice of the occult technique to influence the thinking of the readers and make buyers of them.

A Buddhist priest would never think of trying to persuade a non-believer of his faith to be a follower of the gentle Buddha, but western clergymen throw their energies into winning converts and changing the consciousness of their congregations, in both the social and political areas.

In chemistry, as well as in the Bible, we learned that God

made this universe and left it to struggle along by itself. But He knows what goes on in it from the chirp of the cricket to the movement of the planet in its circle around the sun. Yet he doesn't interfere with freedom of man's individual consciousness. As this is true, then man doesn't have the right to interfere with another's decisions or thoughts.

Despite what Thomas Aquinas decided was truth — that all roads lead to heaven — it is not true. He was wrong in his finalizing a decision on this. Likely he was the victim of some vast astral joke. So many times the homo sapiens are victims of a practical joker from the other worlds.

If anyone should tell you that it is "The Will of God" to change your mind and accept his idea and goal, then you can know for certain this is a sly clever man, or perhaps an ignorant one, who is the tool for some authoritarian.

THE SPIRITUALIZED
CONSCIOUSNESS

Stories about the spiritual consciousness have always impressed me, but one heard in India during my youth left a deep impression and is recalled every time I hear something about the illumined mind.

It seems that during the early days of India a very old wise man always sat by a roadside where pilgrims constantly passed on their way to the tomb of the great Hindu saint. One day a disciple of his argued that perhaps he could become enlightened much quicker by making the pilgrimage too rather than just sitting in meditation, so he joined the parade of pilgrims.

Within a few months he returned very humbled, seated himself beside the old sage, and announced that he was wrong in his decision, that only the ground where his wise old teacher was sitting was sacred and holy. The ancient rishi smilingly said, "God is omnipresent, therefore all grounds are holy and sacred, but it depends upon your realization of His presence, and that is within you, my son!"

55

It took a long time before the real meaning of this little story took hold, but when it did suddenly there was a difference of things in the world. No longer was I viewing life with the eyes of the senses, for all the scales fell away as they did for the lame beggar who asked Peter and John on the temple steps for gold and was told they had none but would give him something greater. Behold, he rose and walked for the first time in his life.

Before we reach this state of spiritualized consciousness, we are usually concerned with the things of this external world, our health, supply and shelter. We rely on food, climate and diet for our welfare, and money for our physical comforts and mental peace.

But once the individual experiences the illumination, he changes his whole outlook on life for now he has reached a realization that wherever he is that is the sacred and holy grounds. The only reliance he has then is on his realization of the divine presence of God within himself.

When lifted out of the physical world to that place we often call the "secret place of the most high," the plane of consciousness which is also known as the fourth dimension of life, we begin to live on the sacred and holy grounds of God where the dependence is not placed on anything or anybody in the external world.

The presence of problems on the physical level is overwhelming. Hardly anyone can succeed in solving these problems through the manipulation of thought. Christ pointed out in his Sermon on the Mount that we cannot grow one cubit or inch by thinking, but by spiritualizing the consciousness.

Frequently we solve a major problem only to find that it has sprung up in some other area of our life. It is only by getting out of this worry belt of the physical world, as one metaphysician once said, that we find freedom from these external problems.

Jesus spoke of going to his father's house to prepare a place for all who wish to follow, for his father's place had many mansions. He meant that those who were desirous of the more abundant life and were bold enough could live in that state of consciousness where the grounds were spiritualized.

Once we enter into this state, the spiritual mansions of Christ, we will find wisdom, power and freedom for ourselves for this is the sacred and holy grounds of the divine presence that the wise old sage spoke about to his disciple. This is wherever anyone may be, but it is only the realization these grounds are holy that makes them so!

ALL ABOUT ECK

THE *SHARIYAT-KI-SUGMAD,*
THE WAY OF THE ETERNAL

The *Shariyat-Ki-Sugmad,* which means the Way of the Eternal, is the ancient scripture of the path of ECKANKAR, the ancient science of Soul travel, or total consciousness.

It is possibly one of the oldest we know about on this earth planet. The Sanskrit writings consist of the Vedas, Upanishads and Mahabharata which can hardly be traced beyond ten thousand years on this planet. The *Shariyat-Ki-Sugmad* is said to be known before the great antediluvian deluge of this world, and beyond, into the hoary years of those so-called mythical continents we know as Lemuria and Atlantis.

The Naacal records are said to be among the first of the religious writings known to us which contain scattered references to ECKANKAR, or total consciousness. Only two monasteries in Tibet, located in the remote mountains, have any of these writings in keeping. These monasteries are so well hidden that it is doubtful that many can find them, not even the Buddhist lamas who have gained the power of moving about the ether at their own volition. The keepers of these records are careful in their guardianship of them. Nobody can enter these monasteries unless first screened by a group of monks who can read the seeker's aura as we can scan a daily newspaper.

However, the *Shariyat-Ki-Sugmad,* which is the guide for those who wish to reach the heavenly kingdom via the route of ECKANKAR, is kept in a golden temple of wisdom and beauty in the spiritual city of Agam Des which lies in the high wilderness of the Hindu Kush mountains in central Asia. Only those who are to travel in the Soul body can reach this strange community of adepts and study the ancient scriptures of Truth.

ECKANKAR is closer to being in its original form than any of the philosophical or religious teachings today. It is neither a religion, philosophy, nor metaphysics, for it is a path to God that we call ECK-Marg, meaning the path of ECKANKAR.

It has been handed down by word of mouth from Rama, the first known saviour who came out of the deep forests of northern Europe. He traveled across to Persia where he paused long enough to give these secret teachings to a few mystics whose descendents were to become the followers of Zoroaster, the Persian sage. Rama proceeded to India where he settled and taught that we could have the experience of God in our own lifetime.

ECKANKAR was revealed to Rama by one of the ancient spiritual travelers. It is likely that he was lifted out of the body and taken to the city of Agam Des where the *Shariyat-Ki-Sugmad* was viewed. Here he had the opportunity to study its contents.

No written instructions had been put down for the followers of ECKANKAR, nor any part of it, until the sixteenth century when Kabir, the Hindu mystic poet, took it upon himself to unwrap the mysteries of the ancient science of Soul travel.

There was a corruption of the original teachings which were by word of mouth and several other paths came out of it, e.g., Shabda Yoga, Magi, Cult of Dionysus, and a few others. Each branched off into its own way as a path to God. Basically the main principle or vital part remains in the form we know as out-of-the-body projection, which is far beyond astral or any of the other lower body movements.

The *Shariyat-Ki-Sugmad* consists of twelve chapters, each about thirty thousand words, made up of cantos or verse in dialogue form. The SUGMAD, God in English, speaks to His chief disciple, Sat Nam, sometimes called the Sat Purusha, the Lord of the Worlds as we know the spiritual plane of Soul, or the fifth region. Many believe He is the Supreme

59

SUGMAD, but he is only the first manifestation of God.

Statements of the highest spiritual nature are attributed to Sat Nam to show that God wants all Souls to be lifted into the heavenly realm again, e.g., *"I am eternal, therefore I am free." "All who come unto Me shall experience the freedom of eternity."*

"Freedom is a completeness within itself for Soul must enter into the divine light, or suffer the effects of the lower reality."

"The true reality is spirit, in any universe of Mine, and he who looks upon it as giving him existence and experience is indeed a wise man."

The ancient manuscript is a true light for the Word of God. It takes up and discusses every phase of life in both the matter worlds and the higher planes. Those who are fortunate to be able to peruse its golden pages are indeed enlightened Souls. Usually it is the spiritual travelers who make it their concern to study this golden book of wisdom and spread its light to those who will listen.

Indeed, as Rebazar Tarzs, the torchbearer of ECKANKAR in the world today, points out, only the courageous and adventurous in spirit ever have the opportunity to see and study its wondrous pages.

THE CONFUSION
IN OUR SPIRITUAL AFFAIRS

The subjects of religion, philosophy, metaphysics and occultism seem to be on a rampage among the peoples of the world in our times.

Truthfully there has never been a more confused state of spiritual affairs than exists in all the topics named in the above paragraph.

The problem of spirituality which is the overall effect of religion, philosophy, metaphysics and occultism is that no two writers or two teachers hardly ever agree upon any point. There are two reasons for this: first, everyone fits knowledge to his own state of consciousness, and second, because of the confusion in semantics which exists in the language of the whole of spiritual subjects.

Strange as it may sound, we all have the tendency to fit any teachings to our spiritual understanding; thus a person with little or lack of knowledge may reject the highest teachings because he doesn't understand. Christ was not accepted by everybody. In fact, he was rejected by the Pharisees and other sects, including the Brahmans of India, so that his life was demanded. This is generally the fate of anyone who tries to break new ground in the spiritual field.

So much of the essentials of the spiritual works comes from the East and brings with it the confusion of various wording of phenomena and aspects whenever Oriental terms are used. But once we brush away the confusion then the concept of the terms becomes clear. For example, that reality we know as God in the Anglo-Saxon language has thousands of names in foreign tongues, e.g., Brahma in Hinduism, Allah by the Moslems, Sat Nam by many of the various sects in India, and SUGMAD by those who follow the path of ECKANKAR. Other names are Akal, Anami, Sat Purusha, Hari Ray and Amma. No wonder there is so much confusion.

We must not be perplexed by words and symbols. We must go to the heart of all things in order to understand the Divine Reality and Its principle of creation and survival. If we do not do this then, frankly, one will continue to wander about until the hardships of life force him into looking for the center of creation of all things. Until he does, this wandering will be a suffering for the individual.

This means that anyone interested in any subject of the spiritual realm must certainly be very careful of how much he reads, studies and participates in meditation, for the simple reason that once he goes beyond a certain point there is no return. It's like a plane flying from Tokyo to San Francisco, when it crosses a certain longitude the pilot must keep going toward his final destination, for now he has passed the point of no return.

This raises the thought that now we are confronted with the problem of what is going to happen to that individual who has crossed this invisible line and moved into the inner realms of the spiritual worlds. Under a competent teacher he is taken care of, but with any teacher who has no experience in the work he is liable to get into areas of trouble.

An example of such troubles can be that too much study of any spiritual works, too much participation in meditation and reading leads to lifting the vibrations of the person. If his vibrations are lifted, and are not under any control by himself or someone who is trying to help, it means that he may become opened as a channel for spirit, and this divine power flowing through him can come through at too strong a vibratory rate.

It means the power has to go somewhere, and like a highly charged electrical bolt it will attack the weakest part of the body. Troubles begin with health and other forms of material problems. The individual affected is greatly puzzled by this phenomenon. He doesn't understand what is going on inside himself. So he continues to put the pressure on for study, practice and meditation, and often prayer, to get out of this situation. But the stronger he does this, the greater become his problems.

Some teachers rationalize this with the fact that he is serving out a karma, or that troubles always come to a person who goes into the field spirituality. Granted that the two reasons are somewhat correct, but they are not always the complete basis for his troubles. Any teacher worth his salt in this field should be able to help the chela gradually unfold so that spirit flows through his follower gently, giving him the proper benefits of both spiritual and material help.

The guru must slow down the vibrations of the chela when they have become too strong. He must keep control of the chela's spiritual actions until the latter is able to fend for himself.

One must be prudent in whatever he does in the field of spirituality for it is a different life from what he lives here

62

within this earth world, and his out-of-the-body awareness often will be of a different nature than he ever expected.

Truth is actually an individual process of consciousness. It depends upon the individual how much he is going to know and learn of it.

MADE WHOLE AGAIN
BY SPIRITUAL HEALING

I was pulled back from death and made whole again by my stepsister who knew the art of spiritual healing when everything else had failed.

Since then I have healed many by the same method she used, with additional knowledge, for that was a long time ago.

Looking back now at what happened it all seems a terrible dream. Long ago when I was five and pleurisy had set in, I was sinking rapidly with a wracking cough and a fever that was burning me like bacon in a skillet. Nobody seemed to know that I was close to death except my stepsister who was proficient in the art of Soul travel.

No attempt had been made to put me in the hospital, but I was getting loads of pills. Nothing was making any headway at this time, and even at that age I was aware that I was not long for this world.

My father was overseas at the time, and our stepmother would not take any action on her own. So it was my stepsister who interceded and saved my life with spiritual healing. She did it by one of the oldest methods, i.e., out-of-the-body projection and healing of the astral body, which reacted upon the physical and made it whole again.

She slipped into my room late that night, which was likely to have been my last one, and sat down beside the bed in the lotus posture, took a couple of deep breaths, and slipped out of her physical form into the Atma Sarup, the Soul body.

She took me out with her, also in the Soul body, and we hung off the ceiling like a pair of eyes viewing the body on the bed below. We were now looking at my astral body which hung upright over the bed. It was like a large x-ray of my human form.

The astral body was filled with a dark, angry flame, and wracked with shudders that might have been from coughing. The furious blaze was located in the left side, just under the heart. She indicated this to me and, impressing me with the thought, she said, "You shall be made whole again."

A wracking pain went through me, but it was gone as quickly as it came. The fire within the astral body simmered down like coals in the deep bunkers of a furnace and died away. A blue and golden light began to glow around the astral body like a deep, illuminated aurora; it was the magnetic aura which shines about all persons.

Instantly I knew that all was well and that the living clay lying on the bed would be my temple again. A feeling of jubilance flowed through me as though it were a river of light. However, there was a dislike to go back into the body again. But my stepsister impressed me that it was necessary.

The next moment I remember awakening to find the family standing by the bed, completely surprised at the swift recovery of their youngest child. Two weeks later when my father returned home I heard him thank my stepsister for saving my life; it seemed that he had projected himself to the house from a far distance, for the same reason, only to find my stepsister taking care of it.

Healing in this manner is one of the oldest arts. Many of the saints, e.g., St. Vincent Ferrer, St. Thomas, St. Theresa, Shamus-i-Tabriz, St. Swithin, Jalal-din-Rumi and hundreds of others too numerous to mention were capable of healing in this manner. The spiritual giants who have walked this earth have mostly been free of human illnesses because of their ability to heal themselves as well as many others. But one thing most of them have done is to heal by use of the Atma Sarup — the Soul body.

Since this first experience I have witnessed many types of healing methods, but none of these, including spirit

64

operation, has had the success of Soul projection.

Nothing is required of the individual who desires to regain his health via those who use the Atma Sarup for healing.

Usually the request is made orally or by letter, however it is not always necessary that the individual make his request in this manner for it has been proven many times that once he puts his mind on the healer or sends out a prayer to the healer, a transformation takes place at once. A miracle happens, transforming him into a being made completely whole again. The healer has received the request via the etheric planes and makes the adjustment at once. Distance is no barrier at all in healing.

In my files are letters from practically every country in the world testifying to the success of this method. Many have never seen a picture of me. Many have had successful healing the moment their letters were dropped in the mails.

A typical excerpt from a letter is, "Since I had an experience of healing on April 23, I have been showing constant improvement. The experience I make reference to was one that came over me suddenly and overwhelmingly. I was in bed and the conviction that I would be made whole came as if from out of nowhere as my mind was not consciously concerned with my state of health. This strong conviction was like a ball of light. It stayed with me for hours, and, as I said, my improvement has been constant since."

This person had suffered for twenty years from a chronic stomach and intestinal condition. But the request was made by a relative without his knowledge until after its mailing.

Many letters confirm healings in a similar manner. A woman was taken to a hospital for a serious operation. It was doubtful that she could survive because of her age, but to the surprise of all she was dismissed in four days and has since been extremely active.

The explanation of this process is simple. Whenever anyone opens himself as a channel for the Holy Spirit to flow through — it doesn't matter where he might be, anywhere in the world, or in other planes or planets — he is able to administer to others. Often he gets into the Atma Sarup and looks at the astral body of those who have made the request for spiritual healing, as my stepsister did for me when she saved my life.

When the problem is located in the astral body, then the Holy Spirit flows through the Soul body of the healer into that of the patient's astral body and the healing is done.

Sometimes the person's aura will show what state of health he is in. Occasionally a letter arriving at my desk carries the aura of the person with it, and I can see what is wrong without having to get into the Atma Sarup to look at the astral body of the person requesting the healing.

There are times when some healing efforts are not responded to, but if the person affected makes the contact in time, the response will be greater. This response is reacted to in several ways — some persons are healed completely in a miracle manner; sometimes the person gets such a spiritual uplift that his unhealthy symptoms no longer bother him. Then there are the ones whose ailments belong to a karmic condition and must be given relief until this state is worked through. The condition must be removed before they can improve.

Healing is only one aspect of ECKANKAR, the secret science of Soul travel. Its primary purpose is to give Soul an opportunity to travel the ancient, secret path to the realm of God where It becomes a co-worker with the Supreme Deity.

RESISTANCE TO
THE SPIRIT OF GOD

Resistance to the Holy Spirit is what brings so many difficulties to the seekers of Truth. Belief in his own lack of understanding which does not see truth in either a partial or whole state is that which gives added karma to anyone who puts himself in the position of not realizing the difference between the states of human consciousness and God-Realization.

It is one of the peculiarities of life that man in his egoistic self does not recognize the fact that when he commits an overt or covert act against anyone who is high on the spiritual scale he is resisting the Holy Spirit. Thus the results of his act will return to him swiftly. The teacher, guru, master, or spiritual traveler who acts as an instrument through which the Holy Spirit flows outwardly is not concerned with what the culprit does for there is no resistance to any malfeasance or hostility toward himself.

An example of this is the case of murders of St. Thomas á Becket, the martyred archbishop of Canterbury, in 1170, who was the victim of King Henry II in a quarrel over the authority of the Church and the State. The four knights whc carried out the assassination of St. Thomas á Becket received the dire punishment of the Holy Spirit. Using the consciousness of the Pope it forced them to give up their properties and fight in the Holy Land for the Cross – a hard sentence indeed for proud men who were captured by the Saracens and lived like lepers for the remainder of their lives.

This is an extreme example of what happens when anyone resists or destroys a channel of the Holy Spirit. History does not record what happened to those who condemned Christ and those who carried out the orders of his crucifixion. But we do know that Pilate, who was responsible for the shifting of the decision to the mob for his death, served out the rest of his life in a state of madness.

Judas committed the grave error of betraying Christ for thirty pieces of silver and gave up his own life by hanging. One cannot sell or betray a channel of the Holy Spirit for materialistic means.

The slightest act against any channel of God comes back swiftly to the doer. This is true even when one gossips and uses malicious talk about the God-Realized people. Personal examples can be given here about those who do not understand the nature of anyone that dwells in the higher consciousness and the troubles that befell them when they attempted to belittle or ridicule the teachings of the blessed channels of God.

The greatest evidence here is that you see the spiritualized ones rise higher, and the maligners go down the survival scale in spirit attitude with a loss of spiritual and worldly goods.

This is not magic in any form which punishes the culprit and gives benefits to the spiritualized ones. No, indeed, it is only the working of the Holy Spirit through the consciousness of those who are willing to let it use them as a channel. This is the danger that the maligner of spirit is up against; for spirit turns away any overt act that is done against its own channel and returns it to the sender. It acts as a protection against the enemies who try to attack its own instruments.

George Fox, founder of Quakerism, gives a long list of what happened to those who persecuted him during his earthly ministry. The list is long and impressive. It should serve as a warning to those who are guilty of such deeds. But man in his human state of consciousness is not impressed and continues to make grave errors that cause him agony, difficulties and more karmic debts.

Christ called his body the Temple of God. But he was actually referring to it as the instrument for the Holy Spirit to flow through into the external world. What he truly said was that every man had the opportunity to become a channel for the Spirit of God to make use of to uplift the world.

Again I reiterate that it is only this Cosmic Spirit which is attacked when one tries to harm the God-Realized. Since the Cosmic Spirit is a law unto itself it has the power to return to the sender whatever he might be sending to the holy essence of life. Thus the Spirit of God in the lower worlds works in a dualistic manner. It can curse the sender or it can bless him. It depends on whatever communication the sender wishes to establish with a person well versed in the spirit-nature of God knowledge.

Whoever keeps a record of such happenings will find that

68

the law of spirit is exacting in its demands for payment. This is actually karma on a much higher level, for when anyone holds a hostile attitude toward a holy person it creates a karmic debt which must be paid for. Even though the impact may be stunning and one of shock, the karma is worked off at once. But often it will stay for many years with the individual who has created the debt.

My own case books show a large number of incidents that have happened over the past years to those who attempted to make attacks on my person. I also saw what happened to several persons who felt the spiritual law in trying to malign Sudar Singh, a high spiritual teacher, my first master, and a member of the ancient order of the Vairagi Adepts of India.

Please remember that the person who is attacked by any hostility and is dwelling in the cosmic state of consciousness is not responsible for whatever happens to the sender of such malignant thoughts or words. He is protected by an amour of light, and the attacker is actually the responsible party and the victim of his own makings.

There is an old spiritual law which must be alluded to here: "No harm can come to anyone unless he so desires it." In other words, when we open our consciousness to harm it will become a part of ourselves and bring injury into our lives. But under the protection of the spirit nothing can injure us in any manner whatsoever.

Therefore we must remember that when we seek to avenge our feelings in some manner or other we are putting ourselves under the law of retribution. To seek to balance the scales of spiritual justice is no guarantee of success to right or wrong. Only the Spirit of God can do that.

Resistance to spirit brings only confusion, unhappiness and disillusion in this world. The stubborn mind is a burden to the carrier of it, but the one who is nonresistant to spirit and welcomes spirit into his life lives in joy and happiness.

TEMPLES OF
GOLDEN WISDOM

The ancient Temples of Golden Wisdom are often the subject of discussion by many who are seeking spiritual truths. But so much of this talk is based on hearsay that legends and myths have grown up about them.

However, those who have had the opportunity to visit any of these magnificent archives of the true wisdom will establish the authenticity of their existence.

There are eight major existing temples of Golden Wisdom in the many worlds of God — two on this planet, one on Venus, and one successively on the astral, causal, mental, etheric, and Soul planes.

These are gathering places for those who travel consciously or unknowingly during sleep. They are usually taken by a spiritual traveler to one of these fountains of knowledge to gather esoteric wisdom.

Many of the spiritual travelers and teachers who formerly lived and served their apprenticeship in the lower worlds have established themselves on the various planes in these ancient temples of wisdom to teach those Souls that visit these places.

These temples are located in the following places and under the guidance of the adepts so named: The Katsupari Monastery in northern Tibet — the Temple of Golden Wisdom under the leadership of Fubbi Quantz, the famed teacher of the sacred scriptures of the *Shariyat-Ki-Sugmad (Way of the Eternal)* and guardian of the first section of these records.

The other school in this physical universe is at Agam Des, the spiritual city in the remote Himalayan mountains. Its name means 'inaccessible world'. We must go in Soul form to listen and study the wisdom here. This temple is called the Temple of Gare-Hira, under the master Yaubl Sacabi, the guardian of that part of the *Shariyat-Ki-Sugmad* which is the sacred scripture on the altar of the inner sanctum. Agam Des is the home of the Eshwar-Khanewale (the God-Eaters) for they partake of the cosmic spirit like we do material foods.

Another Temple of Wisdom is the House of Moksha in the city of Retz on Venus. Master Rami Nuri is in charge of it and that part of the *Shariyat-Ki-Sugmad* placed there.

The School of Wisdom on the astral plane is in the Temple of Askleposis, in the city of Sahasra-Dal-Kanwal. It is under the guidance of Gopal Das, a spiritual traveler in the line of the ECKANKAR mastership, as are all of those who have charge of these wisdom schools.

The next School of Wisdom is in the Temple of Sakapori on the causal plane of the other worlds. It is piloted by that master known as Shamus-i-Tabriz, a Sufi master of several hundred years ago.

On the mental plane is the ancient temple in the city of Mer Kailash. It appears very much like the ancient temple of Diana which was at the city of Antioch (during the Christian era) where once the science of ECKANKAR was taught.

Next is the Temple of Wisdom located in the etheric world in the city of Arhirit. This is under the charge of Lai Tsi, a high Chinese spiritual traveler in the line of the ECKANKAR masters, and one of the faultless guardians of the sacred scriptures placed there for the chelas who venture this far.

The highest of the Golden Wisdom Schools is that of the Temple of the Param Akshar (the House of the Imperishable Knowledge) on the Soul plane. This is the dividing line between the Universal Mind Worlds (the lower regions) and the Spiritual Worlds (the upper regions of God).

The various parts of the great book of the golden wisdom of God mentioned here are parts of the wisdom of the Divine Reality.

The dream method teaching is one way by which those who are looking for truth can visit the various temples. The spiritual traveler will take him out of his physical body nightly to visit the appropriate plane whenever the chela is ready for his spiritual advancement.

The spiritual travelers named here in charge of the

71

different Temples of Golden Wisdom are masters in the field of the ECKANKAR line of mastership. Each is capable of the true initiation which is the spiritual duty of any traveler.

These travelers were once inexperienced Souls like ourselves, but in the course of their spiritual evolution finally reached the heights of the Divine Reality and became the true Satguru and a co-worker with God.

This should give hope to all who enter into the path of God, that which we know as ECKANKAR.

AN ANATOMY
OF SOUL RECORDS

The ability to give readings of the Soul records is a unique skill that very few persons have these days. In the ancient times it was not uncommon, but the art of looking into Soul and learning about its past incarnations is just about lost in our modern era.

We do find, however, that the term "reading of the Akashic records" is very popular. A number of persons are able to read them sufficiently for anyone who wishes to know about his past lives on the physical plane. The Atma or Soul records consist of past incarnations on the physical, astral, causal, mental, etheric and Soul planes. Anyone who can do this type of reading is able to bring light to any lives which Soul has spent in an embodiment in the universal world planes, including the planets.

The reading of the Soul records is the highest that anyone can receive for their own benefit. A person who has the ability to do Soul travel on his own usually has the talent to read the Atma archives. Without casting aspersions on any other type of life readings which are prominent today, we find that the Atma reading is far more revealing for those seeking to know their past lives.

During the first few times in my meetings with Rebazar Tarzs, the Tibetan lama, it was possible to learn to read my own records from the Soul body. One afternoon we were sitting on the side of a mountain slope discussing ECKANKAR, the ancient science of Soul travel, when he asked if I wanted to see how the technique of Soul readings was accomplished.

We both ejected out of the physical body into the higher worlds to the Soul plane (commonly called the fifth plane) where standing beside me in the Atma Sarup (Soul body) he pointed out the millions of past lives of mine. They looked like a fan of playing cards spread over the table and were around my Soul like an arc of pictures.

These Soul embodiments of past lives resembled tiny file cards — each life had a series of these pictures beginning at birth and passing through all events to death, on whatever plane it had embodied itself. We find perhaps several million of these tiny pictures of past lives existing in Soul itself, each with a series on every individual life that we have spent somewhere on some plane within the lower worlds, e.g., physical, astral, causal, mental, etheric and Soul planes.

The Tibetan lama proceeded to show me the individual lives that I had spent on all planes within the lower worlds. All these lives were seen and examined with sharp scrutiny. We were able to look over all the lives needed to be analyzed at the time from this lofty position. We were in the field of total awareness and able to retain a knowledge of what these pictures represented in my long existence in the lower worlds, without looking, as we must do, in the lower worlds of matter, energy, space and time must be considered.

From this lofty position we can see what is in store for ourselves in the future and how to meet or avoid it.

Almost anyone who has become proficient at Soul travel can read the records of those who request it. He bypasses the aberrations of the readee to reach the higher consciousness and give all that is possible to whom he is reading. However, it must be remembered that since these records must be transferred into the physical language via the physical senses, these limitations will be quite a barrier. The reading will have a certain amount of constriction when given and it should be considered in this light.

I have many case histories of readings on individual Soul records in my files, e.g., the case of the person whose desire was to know his incarnations on the other planets of this universe. They were carefully traced out for him showing the various lives he spent on these planets before moving to this earth world. It was shown how he moved from planet to planet during his many lives. He was a member of a superior order of beings who traveled in space ships and in the Atma Sarup.

Another case history was the study of the Soul record of a man's lives on the astral plane between his physical incarnations. It was not a difficult task to read these lives on this particular plane.

This is true of the many other planes that we live upon during our existence between our lives in a lower region. For example, if we are living on the mental plane and reincarnate in the astral instead of the physical, then it is not any more difficult to read these records than any others. It is also possible to read the lives of many who have been out of the physical body for years, such as Socrates and other historical figures.

Anyone stationing himself in the Atma Sarup on the fifth plane can see the past, present and future of another on any plane, if given permission. He does not do this unless requested, for to look at these records of another is a violation of the *spiritual law*. No reader will take it upon himself to do this sort of thing, for he is not granting freedom to the other person.

One must remember that the higher he climbs the spiritual ladder toward the Kingdom of Heaven, the more will he grant others their own freedom and give less interference to another's state of consciousness. As we mount the scale upward the more ethical we become in our conduct. We will not make any attempt to discuss or assist in anyone's problem unless asked to do so, for according to the spiritual law, the individual consciousness of a person is his home — we cannot enter unless invited.

The reader of the Soul records always practices Vairag, the detachment of himself from the emotional and mental states of those for whom he is investigating these records. Under no circumstances can he become involved in the problems of others, except to assist.

Soul records are the most important part of any individual, for all his lives are kept here, not, as believed, in the lower plane bodies. The respective records of lives spent in the various planes may be read provided one can get to the plane above it. For example, the reader must get to the astral plane to read the archives of the incarnations of lives spent on the physical plane, and so on. However, to read any and all correctly, he must project to the Soul world.

Much misinformation can be given from the lower plane readings for we are dealing with maya (illusion) and can often make mistakes that are misleading to the reader.

The only point that I am making here is that anyone who has learned to do Soul travel to any extent can become capable of reading these high records which are stored on the Soul plane, and that certain concepts must be made clear before final entry into the high spiritual worlds.

ASTRAL PROJECTION —
LIMITED OUT-OF-BODY TRAVEL

Astral projection is out of vogue these days simply because it is a limited way of traveling while outside the physical state of consciousness. If one reads enough in the occult and spiritual field he soon learns that astral projection is not at all difficult. There are dozens of books on the subject, and hundreds of articles appearing annually about this type of out-of-the-body physical state travel. But to do Soul travel or go beyond the astral plane is a feat within itself and not many are doing this.

Soul travel can be done by the study of ECKANKAR, the ancient science of total awareness, which puts Soul eventually into the secret realm of God.

We have been impregnated so much with the idea of astral travel that many believe this is the end of out-of-body projection. This does not happen to be true for the student of Soul travel can have perfect freedom. He has the opportunity of visiting any inner plane he wishes, or to make trips to the planets in this universe and the ninety other universes at his own volition.

However, it must be remembered that Soul travel is concerned mainly with the movement of Soul in the lower worlds, the regions from the physical planes to the fifth plane, or what we call the Soul plane. These are the first of those ethereal regions named as the worlds of pure spirit. From there we are within the true kingdom and no longer need movement or travel. Soul is beyond time and space which is existent within the lower planes, such as the physical, astral, causal, mental and etheric planes.

We find that as long as we are within the lower worlds, which are in time and space concepts, we are concerned with travel or movemt, but when we reach the upper planes of God there is no time and space concept. Travel is not needed and we are in the state of total awareness, often called God-Realization or absolute consciousness.

Actually we are working in two fields of endeavor, that of movement via Soul travel and that of total awareness in God. We are involved here with the two states of being, a limited awareness and a total awareness in the Atma Sarup. We are not interested in the various bodies of the lower planes, i.e., physical, astral, causal, mental or etheric, only that of the Soul form.

I find so many people are making the mistake of looking upon Soul travel as other types of traveling outside the physical body a natural mistake, for we have been taught to believe in astral body travel more than any other type of travel out of the human state of consciousness. Astral projection is not too practical except for learning projection as the first step to God. This type of out-of-body movement leads mainly to phenomena. Those who can do astral projection almost never get into the pure astral plane.

All that the path of ECKANKAR does for anyone is to lead him into the Realm of God. This and this alone is the basic goal. If anyone is trying to deal with projection for anything other than this, he is getting into areas of difficulties which will create self-delusion and unhappiness.

Of course many who pass beyond the physical plane at their demise often go into the worlds of the astral plane and find happiness. But we learn, upon examination, that they do not know anything other than this lower realm, which is only the first step to God. They believe this is the ultimate heaven because of the beauty and longevity of the entities living here. However, it means that sooner or later they will have to reincarnate again into a physical body in order to serve out their experiences and to be purified before entering into the true universe of God.

Many who are working with the astral plane masters mistake them for the spiritual travelers. They will be hampered for a while in their search for truth.

I have seen many who believed that the astral plane was the end of all their searching for God simply because they had once visited this realm. They had many interesting reports to make, but it is nothing in comparison to the wonders and glories that come with God-Realization.

There is nothing wrong with astral projection, except that it is a physical phenomenon. We are still in the lower worlds and not working for total consciousness as we should be doing. If one has not set his aim for God-Realization, then he is wasting his time. Any argument in favor of astral projection should be that it gives one the experience of seeing that life extends beyond the physical consciousness. God lies far beyond this plane. Most projection techniques given us by writers who dwell at length upon this subject have us trying to project in the astral body. This is wrong for it means that we are splitting off the sheath of the inner bodies to travel inwardly to the astral plane. This is an unnatural action and could lead to difficulties in the psychic regions. We should go out in the Atma Sarup and take on the astral body when reaching the astral plane. Soul cannot exist on any of the lower planes because of the coarser vibrations unless It is wearing the particular body which is adaptive for the relative plane It is visiting.

While living on the earth plane Soul must wear the physical body, on the astral plane It must wear that body. We should not project to any of these planes in the respective bodies but should project in the Soul body and take on the form of whichever plane we choose to visit.

Any teacher who has learned his spiritual ABCs will not be bothered with psychic phenomena; he is concerned with putting all his efforts on God.

If the Cosmic Spirit which uses him as a clear channel to reach the human consciousness of anyone desires that he should do any particular demonstration of the greater powers of God, it shall be done, but not of his own accord and will. To practice the psychic plane powers he would have to retreat from the higher spiritual planes. In other words, he would fall down the ladder and have to work his way back up.

Whatever we do in the field of Soul travel to get total awareness must be in the ever expanding consciousness of the spiritual self within. Anything other than this will bring a thorny path to travel and the ever increasing idea that astral projection of itself is the source of delusion.

The ultimate is Soul awareness within the realm of God. Unless we are heading for this goal then we should examine our values in life.

The desire to reach the heavenly worlds becomes a strong urging within. Suddenly we find that astral projection is limited to out-of-body travel, then we start seeking the total awareness of ourselves within the true universe of God.

When this is begun with the true desire to find the

Kingdom of Heaven, then all things in our life take on a new light. We find that life is easier to live, that our health has changed for the better, that economic conditions are much less of a problem than ever before, and that difficulties in relationships are righted.

Spirit has now found that we are willing to follow its dictates and flows through us to clear the way for all our lives, not only in this world but the spiritual world as well.

OUT-OF-BODY TEACHINGS
VIA THE DREAM STATE

The master teachings were revealed to me during my early youth by out-of-the-body projection in an amazing revelation via the dream state.

These teachings were brought in a series of dreams by the great mystic, Sudar Singh, at his ashram in Allahabad, India where my stepsister had gone after a two-year stay in Paris studying to be an artist which she never fulfilled in this life. I was taken along with her although fourteen years old at the time and much younger than she.

Sri Sudar Singh, who was a member of the famed Vairagi mystic order of adepts, had his abode in the spiritual city of Agam Des in the western Himalaya mountains. He was a master at instructing his chelas by the dream state, his principal way of teaching. Outwardly he appeared to be a smiling old guru in a deep maroon robe who would sit in silence when meeting with his chelas at his ashram, speaking only when questions were asked of him.

Many of his chelas drifted away because of a lack of understanding about this strange deep-eyed man who seemed to do nothing for them except to give them room and board while they stayed at his ashram.

He would open the consciousness of his chelas provided they were ready and would allow the light of spirit to flow through them. Most of us were too busy with our self-made

79

troubles to see what he was doing — his important work in dream state teaching. He would come to each of us while we were asleep and take us out in our Atma Sarup (the Soul body) into some far corner of the inner planes where he would give us instructions in ECKANKAR, the ancient science of Soul travel.

Often I went with him alone into the higher world where he directed my attention to many things of interest, e.g., the great astral museum where the inventions of this world can be found before they ever reach the human level. Edison is said to have come to this museum via out-of-the-body projection by the dream state. Tesla, Ford, the Wright brothers and many others also found the idea of their creations in this gigantic museum and received credit as the inventors of the things which they brought "back" for the benefit of the human race.

We traveled beyond the astral plane because we moved in the Atma Sarup, which is not limited to the first interplane like the astral body. We found in the city of Sahasra-dal-Kakwal (capital of the astral plane) the Temple of Golden Wisdom where many learn the truths of God so misconstrued on this physical plane.

There is a similar temple in every capital of each plane in the inner worlds up to the true Realm of God. Each has adepts and masters who give the Wisdom of God to those able to reach these respective planes. Not many can reach these planes and, because of this, feel frustrated. Yet if a spiritual traveler like Sri Sudar Singh sees that his chela is ready he takes him out of the sleeping body to sit in groups fortunate enough to have the same opportunity.

The way of doing this is very simple. Trust in a teacher to take care of your inner life until you are able to be on your own, then it is likely you will have the experience of learning by dreams as I did.

It is simple while working with the teacher to be taken out nightly into the other worlds to be taught on different planes. You meet in the first of the light worlds with a teacher whose Atma Sarup is stationed here to link up with you (the chela) in your light body and take you to some respective point in the spirit land to explore or study.

However, one can do some of this on his own if he does not have a teacher who works with him in this manner. Lie down at night and count yourself to sleep. That is, make a postulate that you are going to be asleep by a certain number, e.g., ten or fifteen. Following this you will know that you are going to *"be out"* by the time your physical self falls into a sleep.

Generally you will make the count and drop off to sleep. But almost at once you are awake in the light body standing off in a corner of the room looking at your physical body asleep on the bed. Then you take off for another plane in hopes of finding something that is worth this trouble of traveling in the light body.

You will generally return before morning unless something disturbs your body upon the bed. Often there is a division of consciousness that gives one a dual impression of being both in the physical and in the light body. This dual consciousness is not unusual when practicing the dream technique of inner traveling.

However, you will usually be with a teacher or guide on the inside world, for your progress is always watched so you will not hit any psychic snarls along the way. If allowed, your teacher will make suggestions and steer you in certain directions so that you will get the greatest benefit from these journeys.

THE LONGEVITY OF
THE ANCIENT ADEPTS

One of the greatest mysteries in history is the report of the longevity of the mystics (known as the ancient adepts in the Order of the Vairagis) hidden deeply in the Himalayan mountains along the Tibetan border.

Rebazar Tarzs, the great Tibetan spiritual master, the torchbearer for ECKANKAR (the science of Total Awareness, or Soul travel in this world), is said by many to be well over five hundred years old in his physical body.

He looks to be approximately thirty-five. He is almost six feet tall and walks with a springy stride. A maroon colored robe covers his muscular one hundred-and-eighty five pound frame. His eyes are coal black and his black hair and beard are clipped to a one-inch length.

He is one of the spiritual masters in the descending line of ECK gurus who has inherited the heiratic responsibilities for this planet for those seeking the way to God through ECKANKAR.

Practically everybody living in the physical body desires to be like Rebazar Tarzs — free from pain, disease, and old age. It is an aspiration which grows with the passing years as our ambitions fade on other things. We want to give up all within the human realm and become like the ancient adepts who have lived far beyond the normal span of life.

In examining the history of those spiritual giants who have dwelled among us, we find it filled with examples. St. Anthony of the Desert (fourth century), an ascetic, is reported to have lived beyond 150 years in his physical body. While dying, he requested his 97-year-old companion to fetch his shawl which was at a monastery fifteen miles away. This request was fulfilled by his friend who ran the thirty miles so his master could have some warmth during his last earthly moments.

Most of us with longings for a lengthy life seldom think of the responsibilities that go with it. For example, the adepts of the Vairagis Order (chiefly located in the spiritual city of Agam Des) have the tremendous tasks of working for the uplifting of the human race on this planet and other planet worlds as well.

Rebazar Tarzs has lived one life in one body, but he is one of the youngest in the line of the ECK masters. Many of these adepts are using the same body they were born into many centuries ago. Some have longevity we cannot believe possible. All of them are men and women who seem to still be in the prime of their physical and mental lives.

This is certainly true of those who have reached a degree of spirituality and learned the laws of God. Longevity is a fact well known to anyone who is capable of doing Soul travel. This means he is in control of the physical body and its pressures. He has become a Pinda master with the ability to handle any problem on the physical plane, to confront the body and its senses and the environment in which he has placed himself.

The story of the longevity of St. John the Apostle is one of the most interesting accounts in our spiritual records. No account has been given of his death, though there are detailed stories about the expiration of the other disciples.

Little has been said of him after he wrote the Revelations on the Isle of Patmos, but reports show that he was living during the Middle Ages in a fabulous kingdom in the East under the name of Prester John. This would have made him about 1000 years old.

Having gained a certain amount of ability to do an extension of consciousness beyond the Pinda stage, we find that when awareness is placed on the Soul plane we are able to do many things never before understood and seemingly fantastic. We now become what is known as the Atma Master.

Surely we know that the Wandering Jew, commanded by Christ to remain here on earth in the physical body until He returned, must have become a Pinda Master. He has gone through many transformations, always renewing himself to serve new concepts of physical deathlessness, but always trapped within the realm of matter.

These adepts in the ancient order of ECKANKAR have reached greater heights than the Atma plane. They are proficient in running a physical body while operating on another level. The physical body goes on about its daily routine as if there is nothing at all different in its usual affairs. These are the ECK masters often called the spiritual travelers.

We find that many who are able to do out-of-the-body travel live to a ripe old age for they are spiritual travelers who are keeping their bodies intact for specific reasons.

Among those who were able to live in their physical bodies beyond the average age and keep it in a healthy condition were: Guru Nanak who was said to be over 125 years old before he passed away. Sudar Singh was reported to be approximately 105 years old at the time of his death. The old Chinese master Suto T'sing lived for 267 years in the same body. Fubbi Quantz (an ECK master), head of the Katsupari monastery in the remote Tibetan mountains, is said to be several centuries old, older than Rebazar Tarzs.

These ancients learned the art of good health through projection, one of the distinctive features of ECKANKAR. But it does not mean that we are all going to live like the Green Robe Monks of the Andes, or as long as the Masters of the Far East that Baird Spalding wrote about in his famous series, "Life and Teaching of the Masters of the Far East."

Since many who have learned the extension of consciousness move into higher states, proving that longevity is possible, we find it a fascinating study. We find that Soul travel can be used for self-healing and will take us into the world of good health and prosperity. Not many of us will become like the ancient adepts whose bodies last for centuries because we have no purpose for living this long.

The reason that we wear this physical body for only a few score years is due to our karmic debt. Unless we have disposed of it, we must go from body to body in various incarnations. The next logical factor is that the human race has limited itself in thought form to an individual living our a single life in a short span of years. Neither do we learn to control the body so that it becomes immune to disease and harm. We do not think of going beyond the normal age span like Thomas Parr, the eighteenth century Englishman who lived for 150 years with vigor and vitality.

Should we be fortunate to learn rejuvenation, such as Ayur Vedha, a system of renewing body health, we can at least look and feel 30 years younger. The Kaya Kalp treatment within that system used to bring back youth and health again is given at the Katsupari monastery in Tibet by Fubbi Quantz.

There are also other systems for use to regain youth and health which have proved to be very successful. The only trouble is that they are so well hidden we hardly hear of them. They are more easily followed than the famed drill of the Eshwar-Khanewale, known in English as the God-Eaters.

Actually these are the ancient adepts of the ECK Masters who live in the spiritual city of Agam Des near the border of Northeast India. Some have used their physical bodies for thousands of years and would put the aged citizenry of Hunza down as babes-in-arms. They are able to consume the cosmic spirit for food which preserves their bodies to serve the inhabitants of many planets. Among Christian saints who could do this was St. Catherine of Sienna.

Heading this order of ECK Masters is Yaubl Sacabi whose age beyond human conception. The old men who lived in rural England during the eighteenth century who had defied nature by living from 105 to 135 years seem like trying to compare grandson to grandfather.

St. Germain spent a long time in one body. We have proof enough to know he went beyond two hundred years. He now spends his years in a castle hidden in the wilds of Transylvania.

Madam Blavatsky, who founded the Theosophical Society, acquainted the world with the masters of the White Brotherhood. Koot Hooni, the leader, and many in the order have lived for many centuries. But is is suspected that the line of ECK masters has outlived most of them.

Babaji, head of the Yogoda Satsang Society masters, known in the United States as the Self-Realization Fellowship (under Paramahansa Yogananda) is to continue the work of Kriya Yoga. This is the same reason that Rebazar

Tarzs keeps his own body as an ECK master, to serve the world and the human race in lifting up all to the higher spiritual life.

If we can come to this degree of high realization during our life here, to selflessly serve humanity and its spiritual needs, it stands to reason that we can be purified through God-Realization via an out-of-the-body state of consciousness and keep the physical as a healthy medium with which to bring the message of truth to all in the universe.

THE FUNCTION OF THE SPIRITUAL
TRAVELER IN ONE'S LIFE

Possibly the greatest mistake we have made in the study of spiritual works is to believe that we can use the psychic power to gain what we desire in life.

A worse mistake than this is to think that we can use the pure spiritual power to gain material and spiritual ends.

These beliefs cause much misery in our lives. Many persons have come to me with these mistaken ideas and a hatful of psychic and physical problems. In many cases there is hardly anything to do except to patiently try to get them straightened out so that the pure spiritual power can use them as instruments to spread the light and knowledge to the world.

This is the function of the spiritual travelers, whose whom we know as masters. It is their duty to see that all who seek their help receive a linkup with the Cosmic Spirit so It can use the individual for Its own universal purpose.

This divine power, or whatever name you want to give it, has innate intelligence. It knows what we need and will furnish us with every good that benefits us for the universal cause. It will not serve a selfish purpose. Hence, if we ask for financial help the spirit may bring health instead, for it sees that without health we are unable to find the right position or job to give us financial help.

It will not be directed or pushed in any direction. It works on the same free will theory and independence as we do in our own nature. But so many times people will try to demand something of it or direct it to do something for themselves. It won't reply in any manner and the person trying this becomes confused, upset and frustrated. Very often he does this with the psychic force which is a lower element in this material world. Thinking that he has the answer for himself, he uses this until one day it won't work for him anymore. This is because the psychic force is an inexact science, despite what metaphysics tells us. It is never accurate and most erratic. Whatever we ask for when using the psychic force is found to have a price tag and we must pay for it.

Those who make a study of ECKANKAR as a path to God know that a master will use the power only to assist and lift one into the higher realms of God.

Christ told his disciples this at the Feast of the Passover just before His arrest. Saints, gurus, and all masters, especially those travelers in the line of the ECKANKAR teachers, are fully aware that they themselves are helpless without the divine power. But once It has established Itself within us It uses us as a channel of divine communication.

So the function of the master is to show those who are seeking God-Realization the way toward it. When anyone comes in contact with ECKANKAR and shows no resistance to these works it is then that the link-up with the divine power is given him via the traveler.

The traveler is responsible to God to see that onyone who approaches him to gain truth receives this link-up. It is so subtle, without an outer initiation, the seeker often overlooks it. But he does have the inner initiation via the spiritual senses, maybe in the dream state, or perhaps when the traveler can coax the seeker out of his human state of consciousness into the spiritual state.

Once this initiation has started, Spirit begins to burrow its way through the thickness of the human consciousness much like a drill. Often the reaction from the neophyte is violent because the human consciousness, or negative state, resists Truth entering into it. But the Spirit is gentle in its actions and the change in the individual is less noticeable.

The heavier the human consciousness is the more violent the reaction might be. This is even true of communities, cities and nations. If Spirit starts entering into a community its reactions might be of a somewhat violent nature, for its heaviness in thought atmosphere tries to resist Spirit and the struggle is sometimes more than we anticipate. This is why the path to God is often called the painful and thorny way.

Life for the neophyte starts getting better in every department, and he gains both materially and spiritually. He is led into the right places for his own welfare. Many times he knows that something is working for him but he is too busily engaged in the affairs of the objective world and misses the entire modus operandi of Spirit.

No master will take over the karma of anyone. He knows better for it will destroy his own health and drive him into despair. But he can take the karma of anyone and dissolve it by turning the problems over to the Cosmic Spirit. Neither will he do much for the individual when asked. He may direct the flow of the spiritual power toward that person and it takes on the responsibility of either fulfilling or denying the request. Many times Spirit will fill another need in our life instead of that which we think we need.

The traveler then is the pure channel of God. He is the true instrument, for as Christ put it, "Abide in Me and I abide in you," for he is the present dweller in the Christ consciousness as Jesus was.

He has nothing to do with psychic powers or demonstrations of physical or psychic phenomena. He knows the penalty for using these, and only the use of the spiritual powers will give him a status in heaven.

He allows the Cosmic Spirit to use him and work through him in behalf of all the world. He often does not know what the results will be any more than any one of us would know.

His needs always are fulfilled by the Cosmic Spirit, of course.

For example, a few weeks ago when I needed quiet to do some writing on spiritual matters a bulldozer kept running along the beach in front of the house doing repair work on the breakwater. Its noise was disturbing. I asked the driver to go away, but naturally he didn't pay much attention to such a request. It wasn't but a few minutes before the bulldozer's motor stopped and the driver couldn't get it started again. Just before time to quit it came alive and he was able to get it back to the plant again. Puzzled and angry at the machine, the driver and construction people never had any explanation about what happened.

Spirit was taking care of the situation while I was busy doing something for Its own cause. This is one of the ways that It works when we do not even call upon It for help.

I could give you a hundred or more personal examples of how It works. In some cases I have seen It heal incurable problems in health, purse and human relationships. Once during an altercation with someone over the power of God, I casually point at a tree in a forest that we were driving through, saying, "Look at that tree," but before the sentence could be finished lightning came out of the sky and toppled it in a mighty crash.

I was almost as surprised as my friend. But Spirit needed to prove something to this man, so It used me as a channel to make Its point. There is no need to say that my friend was converted to ECKANKAR, although it took the hard way to do it.

It worked when an airliner wing motor failed at high altitude and we had to turn back to the last airport which we had left only thirty minutes before. I saw Spirit's operation during a trip to the midwest when Chicago had its worst snowstorm in several decades. As stated earlier, whenever anyone who is a channel for Spirit visits communities that have a thick atmosphere of negativism, an attack will be made immediately on this condition to pierce it. In this case the results were so violent that a five-foot snow clogged the

89

roads, airfields and harbors so that all traffic was brought to a halt. Despite this, those vitally interested in ECKANKAR were given a way to get to the lectures there.

We are the instruments through which this divine power flows. It makes anyone who has become a clear channel a master over life and death. It brings good fortune to those who surrender to it, but struggle and hardships will find anyone who resists it.

Spirit will lift us into the glorious heights of the heavenly worlds. It also uplifts and benefits the whole human race whenever we allow ourselves to be the instrument of God. This is our function as spiritual travelers.

THE RAGING DEBATE
OF GOD'S EXISTENCE

The raging debate over God's death certainly has caused a schism between those who claim his demise and those who steadfastly argue that it isn't possible.

Although it has turned out to be little more than a fad for the many who follow the thesis that God is dead, there is a strong element of truth in the statement. That we shall see later in this discussion.

Our problem here is that we are somewhat concerned with semantics of the two powers — those of the negative and spiritual forces — and the three major states of consciousness.

These three major states of consciousness that we are interested in and which we are constantly dealing with are: the Human State of Consciousness, the Self-Realization State of Consciousness, and the God-Consciousness. Once we find ourselves able to exert self-recognition according to these states, we know ourselves and can recognize God ITSELF.

First, in this discussion we must take a look at the mechanics of Spirit. Spirit is divided into two aspects: first, pure spirit which has its home in the God worlds above the fifth plane of the invisible worlds. This is the dividing line between the two grand divisions of the lower worlds and the

90

upper worlds. The negative power, often called the psychic force or universal mind power, has its abode in the lower worlds. This includes the physical plane.

When any person takes up the path to God in a serious manner, the spiritual power from the upper worlds enters into his human state of consciousness to purify this area of consciousness. But the negative power starts a fight to keep it away from its own field of activity.

We can easily call this the perennial battlefield and no man is without it as long as he lives in the human body. It is discussed quite well in the "Bhagavad Gita" in the dialogue that takes place between Krishna and Arjuna.

While in the human state of consciousness we experience pain, anger, doubt, fear, vanity, pride, greed, and other non-survival factors of the lower consciousness.

If Spirit is at all successful in overcoming the negativism within this human state of consciousness Soul can move into the higher level which we call the fifth plane, or the Self-Realization state of consciousness.

By movement into the Self-Realization state of consciousness we have reached the fifth plane of the spiritual worlds where we have freedom and liberation from all in the lower worlds. We gain perception of knowing who we are, where we are going, and what our mission is here on Earth.

This is only a state of spiritual being, gained by Soul travel through the lower planes to the fifth plane where liberation is granted and Soul returns to the physical body for temporary living until the body reaches the end of its life here on the physical plane by natural means or otherwise, which is not of the individual's own doing.

From the Self-Realized state Soul then moves into the God-Realization consciousness where it dwells in Total Awareness. It knows all things, can see all things, and is a part of what we know as God.

When one functions in the Total Awareness state while living in the physical body, he does so in Soul consciousness only. He does not have to travel in this state since there are no time and space concepts involved.

While he dwells in the lower worlds in the Soul Sarup (Soul form) he is in space and time and must be concerned with these concepts for traveling.

This explanation had to be given for it is concerned with the arguments that are flying around about the demise of God.

We must have criterion by which we can judge the actions of those who are putting up such arguments on either side of the issue at stake.

The side that takes the issue that God is dead is speaking somewhat from the human state of consciousness. It is merely a matter of semantics for those to argue this point in a negative manner.

But all who are concerned with this argument forget that every few hundred years there appears a world teacher. In fact, we are never without one, but a new one comes as a messiah or saviour.

Take, for example, the old legend of Pan's death which was shouted throughout the ancient world at the birth of Christ. It meant that a new world saviour had made his appearance to lift the human consciousness into a higher state than the materialistic Pan, the terrifying boy-god of the ancient Greeks.

We must remember that no path to God is of any purpose to us unless there is a living teacher at the head of it. A teacher who can be both the outer and inner teacher to his people who follow this path on which he is the leader.

Therefore we are more interested in looking at the state of consciousness of whoever originated the words, "God is dead" in our times. If he was speaking out of the higher state, it meant that a new way to the Kingdom of Heaven had made its announcement on earth.

Not to be presumptuous, but it was about the same time as this controversial statement was making headlines that ECKANKAR made its latest appearance in the world as a path to God. Whether this proves anything or not, I am not the one to make the judgment. Only history will prove it out.

But the whole argument can be summed up in a few words. The existence of God is only proven to those who live in the higher consciousness.

SPIRITUAL REALIZATION
WILL RESOLVE OUR DIFFICULTIES

In the field of spiritual affairs we find many teachings that are promising material and spiritual rewards — especially resolving difficulties — through different methods.

However, we find that the practitioner of most methods which consist of the manipulation of thought will come to grief after periods of practice for any length of time, i.e., the practioner will fall into one or another thought about failure with the use of these types of methods.

First, he will start thinking that there is something wrong with the system of such teachings which pushes him downward on the survival scale into grief and apathy. He becomes a victim of frustration and defeat.

The other thought is that there is something wrong with the system of such teachings which are supposed to lead him to many gains through practice of these methods. This leads him to running from teacher to teacher trying to examine dozens of systems. Sometimes he is guilty of taking two or more courses from different institutions and reading as many books as he can possibly put his hands on in the hope of gaining material and spiritual rewards through mental and religious sciences.

While there is nothing basically wrong with manipulation of thought to gain a material reward, one must remember that he gets what he goes after; often it is something that is not wanted when the goal is achieved. Also it is wrong to seek parts of the whole instead of the whole which puts the parts together.

Unless one seeks spiritual realization first, he is apt to fail at all material and spiritual goals which he has set for himself.

So many fail to understand this and remain in one pattern of thinking throughout their whole lives. Just before ending their existence here, they admit they were colossal failures in the methods they were trying.

When anyone starts out to solve his problems either materially or spiritually in this way, he is doomed to failure. He may for a little while find himself doing well, but in time he will come to the end of the good cycle and find gigantic obstacles blocking his way. A few can be successful at manipulating the psychic energies to gain success in solving problems; the vast majority cannot.

For some strange reason we have been told that God is willing to reward us for spending time in meditation or trying to use various methods of the imaginative processes to resolve problems. But this is not true for we cannot begin to be successful until we have started reaching the field of the universal worlds — that which is sometimes called the Kingdom of God.

Christ reiterated this many times throughout the gospels by his words, "Seek ye first the Kingdom of Heaven." His Sermon on the Mount is a classic in laying down the basic spiritual law that says we have spiritual realization before all things come to us in a natural way.

No one who has lived on earth in the human consciousness has ever been successful at resolving problems. Not even the many saviours and savants who have trodden among us found the psychic was the ultimate way. They found that problems can only be controlled and never resolved in the physical world. But we must dwell in the spiritual consciousness before true success begins to come to us.

We cannot manage our worldly difficulties successfully unless Soul is able to live again the spiritual consciousness of Itself. In seeking this state of established experience we must first seek self-recognition — what we call self-realization.

The practitioner does not go anywhere, does not seek, nor does he experience anything but recognition of himself. The more he practices the art of self-recognition the greater

94

becomes his awareness of the God State of Realization.

There is no progress or development but rather unfoldment. It is looking deeply into one's self constantly. There is not introversion, which meditation often leads us into, but it is having an objective viewpoint about ourselves.

This is the difference between ECKANKAR and many of the other systems seeking the God State. ECKANKAR uses the simple technique of self-recognition which is sometimes called contemplation, while yoga and other systems use heavy meditation.

Contemplation can be streamlined to the simple explanation of being completely interested in a subject whether we are sitting at a desk working, or in silence. Meditation means concentration for long periods of time.

Westerners are not suited to the meditation methods of the Oriental religions. Our hurried daily pace does not allow us to have time for heavy concentration and long periods of silence outside our jobs. Most of us are not geared for this inner seeking.

Anyone who spends over one-half hour in silence without gaining results should stop and wait until later to make another try. Generally the span of attention will not hold any longer than this, then the mind will begin to jump like a monkey if it is not already doing so.

Too often the writer who has laid down rules for anyone to follow is a professional in the spiritual field, in a manner of speaking, while those who are reading his works are amateurs, or beginners. When they cannot master what he has taught, they feel that something is wrong with themselves for it seems that anyone can follow his instructions.

This is not at all true. The reader or student must find that the system must fit himself, instead of him fitting it, or else it should be discontinued and he should find another one which will.

However, no system will give as complete success as one which shows him how to enter into the Kingdom of Heaven

95

– the spiritual consciousness – and live there through self-recognition.

THE GREAT
SPIRITUAL PROTEST

Occasionally in a letter that comes across my desk, there will be one that shows intolerance of ECKANKAR and all other paths to God, except the one which the writer follows.

This is not unusual for the more we unfold into the higher spiritual life the harder will the negative power struggle to hold its own against the expansion of the individual's state of consciousness.

Consequently we detach ourselves from any criticism, self-assertion and show of psychic powers by others in any form of protest against our way of reaching God.

Seldom do we reply to this type of letter but follow out the basic principles of ECKANKAR. That is, no ECK Master will give direct replies, but lets one learn for himself. For example, once when asking Sudar Singh about the *Shariyat-Ki-Sugmad,* I received a strange reply.

"Rebazar Tarzs once said to me – when I had just asked him a question rather like yours – he said, 'An answer is always a form of death.' "

He was telling me that my question came not from the true spiritual realm. It meant that I was still in the lower state of consciousness and no answer would be accepted regardless of how true it might be. The true answer would come in the form of experience which I would know as being truth. All other answers given would be useless.

When Jesus stood before Pilate and was asked many questions, he skillfully avoided direct answers. But when Pilate asked, "What is Truth?" Jesus merely looked about him without answering. He knew it was useless to give profound answers to Pilate for truth would destroy the questioner.

He also told Pilate, "Thou couldst have no power at all

96

against me, except it were given thee from above."

This is the crux of the spiritual power that every spiritual teacher holds in his hand. He allows freedom to everyone in the midst of a terrible protest against his teachings and works.

Every spiritual teacher has experienced this aggression of the negative power which uses lower consciousness to try to destroy the higher consciousness which has become a channel for the divine spiritual force to use for the uplifting of man.

No Soul has ever reached God-Realization without having been accosted by the lower forces via his fellow man and the elements of nature. It is like a storm that whirls about him, yet seldom does it touch him. It cannot penetrate the spiritual armor wrapped around him and only damages those who make the protests.

It is a great spiritual crime to allow ourselves to fall into the traps of the psychic and physical senses. We fall back into the mental planes and are caught up in the five deadly passions which keep one bound to the wheel of awagawan (the "wheel of the eighty-four").

These five deadly passions are lust, anger, greed, attachment and vanity. When we are intolerant of anyone's religious belief and attitude we have been trapped by the passion of vanity.

The chief function of vanity is to block truth. Any teacher who tells his chelas that he must give up reading, study and listening to others defeats his own purpose. If a chela chooses to leave him for another, it means that either his teachings do not fit the chela, or that the state of consciousness to which the teacher is trying to lift him does not fit.

The true spiritual teacher lets him go without regret for he knows that the chela has not yet reached the understanding needed. He is aware that one goes on hugging his assumptions that all others are mistaken except himself, who believes, "I am right and he who opposes me is wrong. To sustain my belief all others must be destroyed."

It has been this point of view which has created war in the

past, has fermented strife among nations, and resisted all efforts toward enlightenment.

Those who are concerned with protests are basing their attitude upon the conflicts of moral, intellectual or social characteristics. If we break this down it is a feeling of conflict that goes on between mental strife and a feeling of inadequacy. They are constantly moving between two states which brings about a spiritual protest within them, that eventually comes out as vehemence against the teacher for not doing something that fits the desires of the chela.

Seldom does the spiritual teacher answer this type of letter for he knows where the student stands on the ladder to God. He understands the motivation behind the action, and to reply will mean death to the seeker. Only by the chela's own experience will be learn what has happened, and it will not be something that he is apt to forget.

Intolerance is always an aspect of vanity, but there should never be any condemnation for this perversion of the mind. It is something the teacher knows that all chelas must pass through before coming into the true light of God. Only patience and perseverance in the practice of the ECK techniques will overcome this negative quality which fastens itself upon one.

As long as we remember that this lower world is only a place where the negative power reigns and nothing is secure, we are on the right path to God.

NEW CONCEPTS OF THE
GOD-REALIZATION STATE

How many centuries is it since a great religion shook the world? Four immense religions have dominated the Earth planet in the last three years: Hinduism, Buddhism, Christianity and Moslemism.

Now in these modern times we who have been objective about the religions of our day are wondering if they have passed their peak of service to those who desire God and are diminishing to eventually fade away and be replaced by a sweep of another dynamic faith that seizes the people and shocks them into the reality of seeking God again.

During the early years of each great modern religion we can find the records of many who were able to reach the God-Realization state by traveling the spiritual path within the boundary of the particular faith of his own choice. But no longer do we find this exists for most of the clergy and priests have turned to social reforms for mankind. They have put their attention to wars, housing, employment, and many other social questions of the day.

There is no objection to this sort of program, but if one is an astute student of modern religions it will be found that since the beginning of time when a massive religion which served nations and people began reforms for man it started descending the curve toward its demise.

When a church ceases to give God to its audiences audiences then it stops being a religion and is concerned more or less with a program of social reforms. It is a trap established by the Kal (negative) power to lead those who propose to reach the God-Realization state into the illusion that all the works of Soul really belong in the spirito-material universe which includes this physical world.

For centuries prior to the advent of modern religions we find the cults and faiths of the ancient worlds dominating the minds of the masses. But as the consciousness of man grew so the light became greater within himself. He found God-Realization as a natural and growing part of his own being activity. He became more interested in the heavenly worlds than his own physical universe, but knew that he had to live here and accept his worldly responsibilities as long as he was in the flesh.

We find the same situation existing in these times. People are throwing off the shackles of tradition and fidelity to the ideals of orthodox religions and seeking something greater. Many in their ignorance are making a grubby mess of the old esoteric works like Buddhism. The countries behind the Iron

99

Curtain have tried to stamp out religions. The lamas of Tibet are in hiding from the Chinese occupation forces. The masses are gradually sinking into the oblivion of conformity which has been raised above the sacraments of orthodoxy within one's life in these modern times.

The reformers who have come to this world posing as saints and saviours to bring changes in religious, political, social and economic affairs have failed in their missions. They are unknowingly the agents of the Kal (negative) force which rules the lower universes. The greatest mistake the orthodox religions have made is that their hierarchy believes reform of man's affairs in this world is God's design.

We find a vast difference between the ECK masters who have very little interest in this world and the reformers who have posed as masters and saints for centuries. The ECK masters have no interest in the material world except to gather up Souls to take them back again to God, which is their true home.

A deep examination of Truth shows that ECKANKAR, or what we call the ECK, is the root source of all existence. It is the SUGMAD, that supreme deity we know as God. This is the ultimate revelation of Truth!

Therefore, every religion, philosophy and sacred writing since the beginning of time has been the child of ECK, the offshoot of It. Out of It came these orthodox religions to fit the moods and times of the affairs of man.

The ECK serves more than the races of this world. It supports and sustains the entire universe of all universes from God to the lowest plane of the negative ruler, Kal. All beings, all people worship the ECK in some form, be it through the channels of some orthodox religion, cult or creed.

It is the universal ECK, the cosmic message, the God teachings that the present Living ECK Master brings as the message to the races of this world today. He brings to all individuals the living awareness of God so that each will receive the spark of desire to seek out Truth and return to his home in the God realm. Then all things will be right.

100

THE ILLUMINATION OF
THE TRUE SPIRITUAL WORKS

The important thing facing me while in Europe this summer was the enormous hunger for God among the masses of adults. Opposite this was the decline and fall of spiritual values among the young in a society that fails to establish a clear definition of the higher ethics of religion and right living.

The positive and negative values clash not only in that part of the world, but everywhere today. The problem is simple: there is a lack of true spiritual teachings throughout the world despite the fact that the evolution of the human race has been lifted higher spiritually.

Adults are not getting satisfaction from their religious faith and the youth are being misguided by negative values. Too many leaders are telling our youth that they can have freedom through drugs and harmful indigenous ideologies, none of which have any essence of God contained within them.

Freedom of the intellect and scoial behavior is what most people are seeking. But within this is a psychic trap, and few will ever succeed at this goal. It is extraordinary that many university faculty members are without any awareness of God and, consequently, lead their charges toward the above goals.

Those who have sought God and had any degree of realization know there is only one God; that is the highest illumination which gathers in Soul and makes it aware of the secret kingdom of God.

None of the practices that youth may try — meditations, drugs, and pseudo exercises of certain Oriental cults and inane rituals — will lead to God, few if any of the adults will find God, for most are following religions which have only to do with creeds and rites of the universal mind power. Until they go to the heart of the matter, none will find God-Realization.

101

ECKANKAR is the centric channel in the works of God. It is the very heart of the spiritual life by which all live, and it takes hold of all mystic thought even if it is not clearly comprehended. It is the source and power of truth, hence the foundation from which all religions and philosophies have issued. No religious teacher has taught anything else but ECK whether he did so in a diluted form or as the whole truth.

The truth of ECK is that few can give it out in the full sense of totality. Only the ECK masters in the spiritual hierarchy are able to do this as they are able to act as the true, clear channel of God.

Nothing is more depressing than to see the misguided using drugs to extend consciousness, then claiming to have had a God-Realized experience. Nothing could be further from the truth. What the user does not understand is that he has deceived himself and has had only a small experience in the lower astral world. He has become a victim to that destructive mental action we call Kama, or lust, which, if allowed, develops into an abnormal demand becoming destructive and degrading.

In its broader meaning Kama includes all abnormal desires, e.g., drugs, alcoholic drinks, tobacco and exotic foods which are eaten simply for the sake of enjoying the taste. The chief function of Kama, as we see it then, is to pull the user of drugs down to the common level of animals and keep him there.

This is why anyone approaching an ECK master to talk of drugs, or other artificial means for expanding the Soul body, is discouraged or turned away. Truth has never come through such channels. The Supreme Deity will visit Its glory upon Soul only when the latter has been prepared the natural way.

If our world societies are sick do we individually need to be ill? The answer, of course, is no, but we must take upon ourselves the responsibility to follow the path to God regardless of what it might bring us in return — be it suffering, hardship, or whatever.

The illumination of the true spiritual works lies in the

sacred writings of the *Shariyat-Ki-Sugmad (the Way of the Eternal)*. From this holy scripture comes all other sacred writings. Those who have been fortunate to be taken to the Golden Temples of Wisdom and had parts of the *Shariyat-Ki-Sugmad* revealed to them have had a magnificent realization that this is the source from which all truth flows. St. John spoke of it as "the throne out of which the River of God flows" in the Book of Revelation.

Once truth is established in the individual consciousness, we know that the negative values will dissolve. Truth cannot be forced but must enter into us of its own free will. This is why we have sick societies within this world led by those who have accepted the negative virtues to give to the lowly, hungry and sick.

The spiritual works are now entering again into this world to uplift humanity. But we individually must accept our personal responsibility to enter into the full illumination of the secret Kingdom of Heaven.

ECK-VIDYA – THE AKASHA
SCIENCE OF PROPHECY

Prophecy is perhaps the oldest arcane science in the world, accepted by billions of people who have depended on it since the dawn of time through ESP, spiritual mediums, clairvoyants, astrology and oracles.

However, few have ever heard of the ECK-VIDYA – THE AKASHA SCIENCE OF PROPHECY which is the modus operandi used by the adepts of the path of ECKANKAR for delving into the future.

ECK-VIDYA is much more inclusive than astrology or any of the mystical arts that are utilized by the well-known ancients and modern prophets of psychic precognition. It uses more Siddhi powers than the practitioners of prognosis ever dreamt could be possible.

The art of ECK-VIDYA is only an aspect of ECK, which is the fulfillment of the total awareness of God. Prophecy or

103

foreseeing events before they happen, and deja-vu for seeing what already has happened, are on a far wider panorama than any of the lower arts of prophecy.

It can foretell the deeper and more subtle events of life, even to the all-inclusive prophecy of a minute-by-minute mental or physical action to take place in one's life.

ECK is only a path to God, but in its own broad framework are included thirty or more facets, e.g., prophecy, healing, Self-Realization, making events for one's own future, etc. All of these are carried on upon a higher level than those of the occult, metaphysical and religionist teachings. The vibrations of anyone practicing ECK-VIDYA are so high that those on the lower spiritual scales never can be compared with them.

The ancient mysteries were established upon the keystone of prediction. The Elysian, Orphesan, Pythagorian and many other ancient mystery schools had initiations which consisted of the chief priest going into a trance and giving predictions for those receiving instruction into their particular cult. Most of the works with which members of a mystery school were concerned were predictions on some basis or another.

The foundation of the argument against Socrates during his trial was that he was giving the youth of Athens false hopes by predicting the political and material future of individual persons and of the chief Grecian city.

The most famous of all mystery cults in ancient times was the Oracle of Delphi in the Temple of Apollo at Delphi. During a visit to this famous oracle, which is now one of the great tourist sights of ancient ruins, I met an old man who claimed that it still speaks to those who have the gift of prophecy and divine insight. At first his words were taken lightly until, while sitting alone on the great pile of ruins near what was the mouth of the oracle, I heard its words come slowly and distinctively. When the first shock of surprise had passed, and I had slowly digested what was said, it was clear that the ancient gods of Greece still lives for those who had the ears to listen. Shortly afterwards I began the practice of ECK-VIDYA.

104

The other oracle at the Shrine of Dionysus, located on the island of Delos, was one of the great sites of ancient prophecy.

However, the oracle which was still active up until the early part of this century was hidden deeply in the wild mountain ranges of northern Tibet. It is known as the Voice of Tirmir.

I visited the oracle twice with Rebazar Tarzs. The first time I was initiated into the Ancient Order of the ECK Adepts. The next time was to confirm some of the prophecies of my mission in this life.

The oracle is one of the oldest on this planet and was used until about fifty years ago by the ECK masters when initiating chelas into their order.

A few use the hoary modus operandi via the ECK-VIDYA method of giving prophecy for those who wish to know their future. The old instructions of divination which were handed down are gone. Those Tibetan masters who were able to use the ECK-VIDYA way of looking into the future have dwindled to a handful, headed by Fubbi Quantz, the Abbot of the Katsupari Monastery near the old site of the Voice of Tirmir.

The ECK-VIDYA method of reading the akasha records is not simple. The chela or student places himself under the tutelage of an ECK guru, following his instructions to the letter. By constant contemplation, coupled with strong spiritual shocks, the chela is able to awaken the Tisra Til (the spiritual eye) and bring about the release of the Atma Sarup (the Soul body) from the physical body, putting it above the realm of time and space.

This action leads the Atma Sarup upward and through the other planes until it has reached the culminating experience of Moksha or Samadhi — that which we know in the west as Cosmic Consciousness (known in the circles of the ECK adepts as the ECKSHAR).

When at this position, one knows all his future and the future of others if he so desires.

Generally one does not induce the trance state to leave the body, but can do it by what is called among the ECK adepts as the Saguna Sati. We would know it as instant projection, the ability to move at will out of the body into any of the higher states of consciousness.

I can do this by simply concentrating on a physical object for a few seconds while repeating the secret name of God. There is usually a ping within my head. But if often sounds as loud as a mortar gun. I find myself hovering above the area we know as time and space looking at what might be in store for anyone who has asked to know about his future.

ECK-VIDYA actually means total knowledge. All that comes to him who can read the Akasha records via the Soul body is that which is known as Divine.

The practice of the ECK-VIDYA has nothing to do with the practice of yoga, spiritualism, drugs, Vedanta, astrology or any kind of Oriental rituals. We are not concerned with the asanas (postures), mantra (chants and vibrations), mudras (gestures and binds), and pranayama. Neither does it have any relationship with the intellect or study in philosophies.

ECK-VIDYA works on the principle that the world is interlocking and is a unity which can be observed once we lift ourselves above the regions of time and space. From within this position we are able to see all as a totality and to sort out the powerful magnetic fields around those for whom we are reading.

One can be in the midst of a group of people and still put himself into the state of higher consciousness. The physical body will continue to function.

Last summer, while in London, I was invited to the home of one of the British ministers. Knowing my abilities, this official asked several confidential questions about what the future held for the foreign affairs of the nation. I told him about the coming trouble with China, also about the economy shift that the Prime Minister was to make in dropping several cabinet posts and taking over the duties.

However, the goal of ECK is not to develop the acquisition

of Siddhis or supernormal power of this nature. ECK-VIDYA is only an aspect of this enormous path to GOD.

Generally speaking, ECK-VIDYA is the achievement of spiritual insight with whick to look into one's own future on a minute-to-minute basis or day-by-day readings.

This is the realization of the great works of the Divine Deity in our lives which can be applied to all things and events we meet in the everyday routine of living.

One should never be side-tracked from the Ultimate Realization with GOD. Our values change as our recognition of the inner strength and relationship to GOD occur.

ASTROLOGY, REINCARNATION
AND KARMA

Astrology, Reincarnation and Karma — trinity of higher levels of the spiritual science. It definitely has its place in the teachings of ECKANKAR.

Each of these three aspects of the trinity is an exacting science since Soul must serve in the lower worlds in order to gain spiritual purification. So ECKANKAR is concerned with all three of these spiritual sciences.

It says in the *Shariyat-Ki-Sugmad (the Way of the Eternal),* the holy scripture for those following the path of ECK, that we are in this physical universe to gain spiritual experience.

God sent us here from out of the heavenly kingdom as untried Souls to gain spiritual purification. We are like children who must attend school to prepare us for a place in the world.

The lower worlds, which are below the Soul plane, were established as a training school for Soul. It is created in the heavenly world and sent into the lower worlds to receive Its spiritual education. Eventually, after many incarnations, Soul is purified by Its experiences after ridding itself of the lower universe karma, via reincarnations on the Wheel of the Eighty-Four.

107

The Wheel of the Eighty-Four is the zodiac where we must spend so many incarnations in each sign in order to overcome the influences of the zodiac signs. When we have conquered the Awagawan, which is the Wheel of the Eighty-Four, we return to the heavenly world with the guidance of a spiritual traveler.

After Its return to the heavenly kingdom Soul is able to serve with God as a co-worker in the various planes of the worlds which make up the total universe of the Supreme Deity because it has gained spiritual judgment and maturity.

It is said that each Soul after leaving the Kingdom of God in the beginning of Its life will have rounds of births and deaths in the lower plane, mainly the Earth world. This includes the various species of living beings that It must pass through to the human apex and Its many lives in the latter form.

The eighty-four on the Wheel means the number of times we will have births and deaths in the lower worlds. Eighty-four lacs amounts up to eight million, four hundred thousand times, and a lac equals one hundred thousand. In other words, the individual Soul will go through each zodiac sign seven times in order to be able to conquer the influences outside itself.

This is true but there is the accelerated way of getting through this karma so one does not have to spend his time in a round of births and deaths. This is the path of ECKANKAR which leads to Total Consciousness of GOD.

The influences as reported by astrologists exert tremendous pressure on Soul so long as it uses a physical body. Much of the karma that we are working out is that which is natural in any given sign of the zodiac. As quickly as one learns to overcome the influences of one sign he moves into the next. This may be done anywhere, whether on the Earth planet or any of the other planets.

Following this, Soul moves on to the next plane, i.e., the astral, where It will go through a different process until It has reached the end of Its period there. After this, It spends time in the causal plane, and then the mental world. When It is through with all of these, It enters again into the heavenly worlds as a pure spiritual entity to serve God.

However, those who are able to find the ECK masters and follow the true teachings will be able to get off the Wheel of the Eighty-Four.

The ECK Master will show the chela the simpler way of getting into the God-Realization state which will cut through all the illusions that the negative forces try to snare him with.

Any teaching which informs us that Soul must spend its time as allotted for eight million years or more within the lower worlds is not of the truth.

Since ECK encompasses all the teachings of religions and philosophies it serves to lift Soul into Self-Realization and later to the true God-Consciousness where liberation is found.

There is so much to discuss about the three aspects of the spiritual sciences — astrology, reincarnation and karma.

So much is to be given out to the world about ECKANKAR and its path to the Supreme Deity that it is doubtful that any one person can do it within the years he has in this world. But if he is an ECK Master then the teachings go on in an ever-widening circle from the planes beyond until they take in the whole lower world.

UFOs ARE VISITORS
FROM ASTRAL PLANES

Official investigation of UFOs by a government project at the University of Colorado is due to fail, for these phenomena, generally believed to be visitors from outer space, are only astral plane entities.

This explains why some persons are able to see flying saucers and other UFOs while others cannot. UFOs consist mainly of astral projections (as explained in my book, "The Tiger's Fang") from that plane which resemble physical objects so closely that many who see them call such phenomena visitors from other planets.

People see them; animals are aware of them, and while in no sense "unnatural" they are, of course (being projections), only seemingly real and solid. Flaming engines roar, red and green lights flash, and they move with incredible speed — but only in the minds of those who project and receive the images.

Anyone who is a follower of ECKANKAR is aware of this. He knows what goes on in those planes beyond the physical universe. Unlike most people, followers of ECKANKAR do not take the UFO experiences at face value. They are acutely aware that "things are not what they seem."

ECK travelers are cognizant of the psychic planes above the physical universe, i.e., the astral, causal, mental, etheric and the Soul plane which is the dividing line between the worlds of the heavenly realm and the lower psychic ones.

These lower planes are not actually separated from the physical universe; they co-exist with it. The two of them (physical and psychic) exist not alone but relative to one another.

The logical explanation for UFOs is that they are not visitors from outer space, secret developments by any government, nor the result of mass hysteria. They are perfectly natural astral projections of the psychic world.

ECK travelers who make daily journeys into the other worlds are warned at the start of their training on the inner planes what to expect from the snares and traps of the psychic powers. UFOs are one of the phenomena objects they will witness, but they are to give them little attention and proceed onward to eventually reach the fifth or Soul plane where they will be liberated from all the trials and troubles of the psychic and physical worlds.

The UFO experience is generally a subjective one, something like religious or emotional occurrences.

These two planes often impinge on one another and physical manifestations are also numerous in the astral plane.

110

Many who have never ascended above the physical plane have the intuitive ability to see such manifestations as UFOs. This explains why, when a UFO is sighted some people in the immediate vicinity will notice it, but not others. There are any number of cases of UFOs appearing over large cities in the daylight hours to be reported by only one or a very few people. In one case, a youth called the police to a farm and the two officers saw the UFO rise over the farmland. Horses in a nearby corral were disturbed, but the farmer and his family were unaware of the proceedings. This sort of example could be expanded without limit.

Ezekiel saw a "wheel" not a rocket ship or a flying saucer because in his day the human mind was not able to conceive of such things. At that period the wheel represented the ultimate in technology. UFOs in the Middle Ages suspiciously resembled air balloons. Those of the late nineteenth century were reported as having gondolas beneath elliptical bodies and their engines went chug-chug — not whoosh!

Those who project the amazingly lifelike UFO image from the astral plane are not actually very spiritually advanced. They can only project what they have heard about, and their imagery is not the best, or they would be aware of and interested in reaching the God plane where Total Awareness would be found.

Those who do see UFOs generally have a high I.Q. and possess some clairvoyance which gives them an insight that others do not have.

If only they would reach on further it would be found that any ECK spiritual master would come to their aid and guide them past this phenomenon toward the highest realm of God via the path of ECKANKAR.

INITIATION – ITS PLACE
IN OUR SPIRITUAL GROWTH

Initiation into any secret spiritual society is the supreme distinction for anyone seeking the realm of God. Passing through the initiation ritual brings the manifestation of the sacred forces and lifts each into the transcendental realities of God.

However, the initiation must be given by a true spiritual master who links the chela with the spiritual forces and gives him freedom and liberation of Soul. This is the basic key to initiation in ECKANKAR, its place in our spiritual growth.

Not everybody is ready for initiation, but many teachers of the esoteric subjects who arrive on these shores from the Orient make little distinction as to who has reached a climax of growth and is ready for initiation. Usually the initiation is given first and the study of the respective teacher's work comes second.

This is the wrong way of handling initiation; it is little more than joining any orthodox cult or religion with a ritual of some nature. Study for the chela who is following the path of ECKANKAR must go on for two years before he can qualify. By this time the chela has learned enough about ECK to determine if he wishes to follow this path. Should he decide against it, there is always the freedom to leave and find another way to God without opposition or mental qualms.

We find that anyone who takes up the study of ECKANKAR will be given an inner initiation when he begins to practice the spiritual exercises of ECK laid down in the first series of discourses called "The Precepts of ECKANKAR." He may not be aware of it, but the changes of this inner initiation which are made in him are noted by the master and friends. Some chelas do have a vivid recall of the inner initiation, but others have no feeling or understanding of it.

This inner initiation is sometimes given in the dream state

by that entity whom we call the Dream Master. Often it is given while the chela is fully conscious and can remember everything about it. It is truly a wonderful experience for those who can recall every part of this first initiation.

An inner initiation is made possible for the purpose of gradually preparing the chela for the final link-up with the Sound Current, the audible life stream — that which we know as the Word, spoken of so much in the Bible and other sacred literature.

Upon finishing the second series of discourses entitled "Soul Travel — The Illuminated Way", the chela is ready for the second but objective initiation which is the one which gives him the secret word for himself. This word is not a mantra but fits his vibrations with that of the spiritual power. He then is an accepted member of the Initiates of ECK.

Following his second initiation he is given further studies and later the ninth initiation which brings him into the Secret Order of the Vairagi, the Brotherhood of the ECKANKAR Adepts. He is accepted and able to do almost anything that they are capable of doing.

There are twelve initiations in the works of ECKANKAR. It takes several years of study for anyone to reach the pinnacle area where he can become a true co-worker with God in this lifetime. But once the chelas have passed the second initiation much of their karmic debt has begun to work off swiftly. They never have to return to the Earth planet unless they so desire.

Our greatest obstacle lies in the fact that many teachers want those who show any interest in their respective works to be initiated at once. Such an initiation may do more harm than good for the chela. Seldom does a chela have any experience in esoteric affairs, and most lack a knowledge of what is in store with such initiations. Often they become dependent upon the teacher rather than learning what can be done for themselves. They feel that to leave the teacher would cause spiritual damage, although they may not be getting anything from the studies of these particular works.

113

Many teachers of this nature also discourage the chela from leaving after initiation into their path of God with fear techniques, e.g., that if he does leave the studies they are teaching he is doomed to remain on the astral plane and never have any spiritual growth. This is interfering with the chela's freedom.

There is also too much promise of what an initiation may do for the chela. Those who seek it may expect the glories of God at once, according to many teachers. Also their physical and economic welfare will be taken care of by some mysterious means of God. These promises are not completely truthful. Whatever the chela gets out of an initiation will depend entirely on himself.

He cannot under any circumstances get anything greater than his own spiritual unfoldment demands. This is the crux of the whole teaching of ECKANKAR. One would not expect to become a highly evolved engineer should his talents be developed for music. Not that it isn't possible, but he is not likely to succeed because of lack of interest plus other factors.

This is especially true in the spiritual works. Too many times a wife or husband will practically twist the mate's arm to become interested in the same studies. This is foolish because we find that while one is spiritually unfolded to certain levels, the other mate is not. Therefore the best thing to do is to leave the uninterested mate alone.

This situation offers a problem to the master when the initiation is to be given to one member of a married couple and the other has no interest. The master should explain to the chela that he must discuss the initiation with his mate before it is given. If an agreement is reached between the two parties involved, initiation is then made possible for the one who requested it. However should the other mate desire also to have the initiation with the chela who requested it, the request should be granted although he may not have the prescribed requirement.

One of the purposes of the spiritual path is to keep the

family intact, not to separate it, and if those within a family are going to withdraw into themselves or to try to force others within the family unit to take the same path they should drop it and take a way which is agreed upon by one another.

The initiations in ECK are the oldest of any secret society. They have been used since the dawn of time. The citizens of the spiritual city of Agam Des in the western Himalayas are initiates on the path of ECK. These are the Eshwar-Khanewale, or what we know in English as the God-Eaters, those who consume the cosmic energy instead of material food.

When the chela has advanced to the third initiation he is able to visit this city ruled by the benevolent ECK master Yaubl Sacabi. As he travels onward into the heart of God the chela will pass through further initiations, each one a test, until he has finally entered into the Total Awareness of the SUGMAD, the secret kingdom of God.

Some of the tests are given by the ECK masters, the keepers of the *Shariyat-Ki-Sugmad* in the Golden Wisdom Temples on the different planes where the chela studies. These masters determine when the chela is ready for study on the next higher plane, where he will take up advanced work of ECK. When he has developed to a certain level and is ready to go to the Golden Wisdom Temple the master gives him an initiation which will send him into the higher realms.

If anyone desires to give an initiation to a chela which keeps him in the lower levels, like the transcendental meditation technique, or those which are concerned with only self-realization, or the universal mind, then the teacher is doing the chela a disfavor. He will have little advancement on the spiritual path. Mantra yoga will not carry anyone further than the mental plane, despite the claims made by the practitioners and teachers in their field.

Often the leaders in mantra yoga will speak of the realm of pure thought, but this only reveals their arena of operation. They are not working on the true spiritual planes, but in the realm of the mental worlds where the negative power is still king.

Neither do the advocates of self-realization bring lasting peace for they are only reaching the Soul plane (fifth plane) where the knowledge is that of self-realization. Again this is not reaching the God-Realization state. Self-realization is self-knowledge, and God-Realization is God knowledge.

We find that when anyone requires a stipend in any monetary way for initiation, he is breaking the spiritual law. No true spiritual master asks anything for an initiation. He gives from the love of giving and expects nothing in return.

No remuneration is expected from the chela to receive the initiations in ECK. After he receives the second initiation he is entitled to a series of monthly letters called the Wisdom Notes, which are for the initiates alone. He takes up the study of the *Shariyat-Ki-Sugmad* because he has advanced this far in his spiritual unfoldment.

Until one has earned this right he is still under the law of karma and must work with its exacting demands of compensation.

THE IMPOTENCY OF MEDITATION
AS A WAY OF ENLIGHTENMENT

Meditation, like prayer, has been a traditional ritual in religious and philosophical circles. It is perhaps one spiritual method of seeking God enlightenment which has been a universal failure, especially with the Occidental seekers of light.

This is practically heresy to those who have been steeped in this orthodox method of seeking realization of any spiritual nature. Yet the statement is true due to the fact that we in the Occidental world have been grossly misled about the Hindu religious methods of worship, not only by the Indians but generally by the westerners who are leaders in the religious and philosophical fields.

Meditation is a word that fits almost every technique which is used for seeking God-Realization. But the word as we are using it here means sitting in passive silence awaiting the descent of God's light into the practitioner. This is the Hindu religious way of meditation. But sitting in the silence and doing nothing certainly does not create an atmosphere of activity. It tends to make the participant a more passive person and if practiced enough he will come close to a state of neurosis.

This has been established in the fields of psychology and psychiatry as a truth. It has become known that many people who have turned to meditation as given by the Orientals have reached a state of ill health and were compelled to seek medical attention.

We find a difference between the followers of the traditional Hindu religious meditation methods and those who are practitioners of the spiritual exercises of ECKANKAR. The difference is that so many who try to practice meditation are not prepared for it and will sooner or later become the effects of their own efforts.

We also find that this type of meditation will bring little more than visions which must be separated to tell reality from the pseudo. So many of these visions are within the practitioner's own little universe! But they are accepted as something sent by the Supreme Deity as part of the universal worlds as a reward for the practitioner's faith and devotion in keeping to his periods of meditation.

This self-deception is not always the fault of the practitioner, for he has nothing by which to measure these subjective experiences. Thus he must accept them as truth because he does not know any better.

The spiritual exercises of ECKANKAR give their own participants a "yardstick" to measure whether the reality gained from out-of-the-body consciousness is truth. Those practicing these exercises are able to gain judgment and discrimination about their own abilities to travel into the other worlds and their experiences for survival of Soul.

117

This is the main difference between the spiritual exercises of ECKANKAR and the meditation practice of the Hindu religion. Those who practice ECKANKAR are able to travel to the Godhead and return to the physical body. Those who practice meditation are only able to create some condition by which they hope the attributes of the Godhead will descend into themselves within the physical body.

Meditation is merely a passive state in which one tries to draw the light into himself while sitting in a position called the Asana which is one's posture for trying to attain oneness with the Light and Sound forces.

Nothing comes of using this method because we are dealing here with a situation which is for specialists, these being the ones who have worked with this method for many years, usually from childhood, and have lived in a climate that is conducive to their thinking and feeling toward God-Realization.

I am speaking here of the Oriental holy men who are able to withstand austerities by living in remote places, especially caves in the high Himalayas. By their long periods of silence and ability to do without food and the normal comforts of life they attain some success with the meditation method as an unfolding toward God.

It is certainly true that few Occidentals can succeed at such a path to God because we are not conditioned to the Herculean tasks of such monstrous concentrative periods. If a man puts himself into silence for fifteen years or more he certainly has an endurance beyond the capacity of normal people. But to what purpose?

If he withdraws from life what does he gain by his austerities and lack of social contact? The usual claim is that he is in contact with God. If this be true then why didn't the Anchorites of the fourth and fifth centuries after Christ add something to the spiritual development of mankind and the sacred writings of the church?

None of these people who choose to suffer hardships in silence in the name of God make any worthwhile spiritual records for us to follow. In my own personal research it's been found that those who claim to have spent long periods in silence and to have come out of it with great truths give us pause to wonder at what they claim to have discovered. Frankly, most of what they have found within these periods of silence, after years of it, was something that might have already been known to a small segment of the public at large.

In one case particularly it was found that the leader of a popular religious cult claimed to have discovered a new transcendental meditation technique after spending sixteen years in meditative silence. What he had to give after this unusually long period away from social contact only turned out to be a mental method which was generally well known among well-informed students in the spiritual fields. One asks himself of what good then is it to spend such tremendous time in meditation if he is not to gain some God-light and wisdom?

The purpose of man is to live here on Earth in a dual role. He is both spiritual and physical and cannot live entirely as either so long as he is encased in the temple of flesh. He will be able to rise into the God-State and remain there for a time and then must descend again into the human state of consciousness. It is only when we are able to get beyond this physical life, after death, that it is possible to rise into the God-State of consciousness and remain there. But we must prepare for this by learning to project ourselves into it and dwelling there temporarily while living in the flesh so we will be able to reach the secret kingdom for permanent residence following demise of the human body.

This is why meditation will not resolve the condition of God-consciousness for any of us while in the body. The spiritual exercises of ECK are the only path that will give us the opportunity of entering into the God-State temporarily while in the human body.

These exercises are not at all conducive to passive action. It is true that the practitioner of ECK sits still while doing the exercises, but we know that there is still action about them. We leave this state of consciousness and go into another plane leaving the physical body so that we can receive the light and sound forces which flow down into the body via Soul which is out in the invisible worlds and which is acting as a channel for these twin powers of God.

The very difference here between the two systems is that the meditation technique does not enable the individual to leave the physical state. He receives the light into himself, that is — the physical body, directly in the meditation period. Often this cosmic light is so strong that it will wreck the body in the same way as too much electrical voltage. In time the body will be broken down and ill health results. Should we study the lives of many saints who believed that meditation was the proper path to God it would be found they all passed away in bad health. But those practicing the methods of ECK or similar ones were healthy far beyond their years and had an unusual longevity.

As just stated, those capable of leaving their physical bodies and receiving the light via the Atma Sarup (Soul body) will have longevity and good health. All benefits which we have expected in life will come to us and eventually we will return to the heavenly kingdom and become co-workers with God.

MEDITATION: EASTERN VS. ECKANKAR

Meditation is making use of the feminine principle in order to reach the Godhead. It is part of the duality of the lower worlds, and that with which we will be making contact unless we recognize it in time. We find that the use of this method over a long period of time tends to make the users of it more effeminate than ever. The users of the ECK exercises will grow in strength and freedom.

The mistaken idea that many have in the use of the techniques of meditation is that we grow more godlike in nature. Since God is neither feminine nor masculine of ITSELF, then we are falling into the trap of the negative power which throws up the illusions of misunderstanding.We cannot go any further than the mental plane with the meditation technique; therefore the use of it still confines us to the lower worlds.

If we should take a look at the state of the Oriental countries, their wisdom does not seem to have been very effective at home. They appear to be in a greater state of confusion than those in the Occidental world.

Therefore we must realize that most of the Eastern religious teachings, like their other ways of life, are in any case clearly designed for the Eastern way of living — for countries where a hot climate and general poverty is conducive to contemplation inactivity.

These teachings work even less effectively in the Western countries where the cultural traditions are outward-looking, active and optimistic. Except for a few holy men we find the usual Oriental character much like that of the nations of the rest of the world, which includes such traits as selfishness, hypocrisy, arrogance, immaturity and materialism. A few are living in wealth and comfort while the masses are starving.

They are different from the western people because their world has burdened them with different problems. Their climate, with inescapable yearly cycles of flood and drought, has fostered the world's gloomiest religion. Centuries of undernourishment have left them with weak bodies, and they expect to live only about half the years we do.

Therefore, their holy men have developed the passive meditation state which is good for their followers because it tends to deal with the problems of escape. In principle it is the same as one reading for the purpose of getting away from the reality of life. It simply cannot be done, for no matter how much time we spend in meditation and what airy feelings are received in this state it does not resolve the problems of having to face the affairs of the day in this world.

One highly respected spiritual leader stated not long ago in a pulpit that it was ridiculous that the Beatles and many

121

others had to go the East in order to try to learn about God. They should have been sent there because they represent life, love, success and happiness. All that the East represents is starvation, misery and a few creditable spiritual teachers, but there is only one avatar and one path, and he is not in India. What they will find is hardly worth the time because it will be a pseudo-spirituality which is hiding a vast amount of materialism.

This is the trap that the unwary fall into, those who have not had experience in the spiritual ways of life. The same results can be gained in a church ritual as in the meditation act, only an emotional uplift against which sooner or later the body will cause a rebellion. Then it will show evidence of those karmic effects, as in the case of Ramakrishna, the new prophet of India, who died early in life of throat cancer.

Therefore we find that meditation is not fitted for the Western nature. We must learn to use the spiritual exercises of ECK which bring about enlightenment by lifting Soul beyond any of the spirito-material planes, such as the astral, causal, and mental. The worlds of the lower planes, such as these just named, are not considered in the works of ECK except to pass through into the Godhead.

Many people who come to me say they do not want to be bothered with the lower worlds but want to make direct contact with God. They are simply not willing to go through the preparation to enter into the finality of the Absolute.

Meditation brings one into the mental plane where the user becomes one with all things. Those who practice the spiritual exercises of ECK learn that one does not become one with God, and doesn't have the established union with God as claimed by the Hindu religionists but becomes a co-worker with the Supreme Deity.

There is a vast difference in this — for being one with God we are living in a passive, useless state, but as a co-worker with God we are the active worker with a divine mission to be re-established somewhere in the universes of the spiritual kingdom to do our spiritual assignment for and with the

Supreme Deity as described in the *Shariyat-Ki-Sugmad,* the sacred writings of those who follow ECKANKAR.

IS THE NEW AGE MESSIAH
IN OUR MIDST?

The question of the new age Messiah has been one which is under constant discussion by those who are directly interested in spiritual and religious matters of the present times. The whole point which is being presented here is whether the Messiah for this present age has made his appearance, and how do we judge whether he is with us now. Certain factors and events which are coming about somewhat prove that we are blessed with his presence.

Since the advent of ECKANKAR into the modern world, starting about 1935, the crises in human affairs have become more intense and now seem at the bursting point. It appears that this ancient teaching which has made its way back into the attention of the world, after lying dormant for centuries, is here for a purpose. That is to bring a stronger spiritual strength to all those who become its followers.

The Ancient One, the agent of God, whom we call the Messiah, or the Godman, appears in the world with every new age. Now he has appeared with the age-old teachings of ECK, which will give the human race a spiritual boost, taking many over the crises into the realm of God. The way will be perfectly clear now that many can see where the path of God is leading them.

The Buddhist scriptures speak of Maitreya who comes for this age to take the followers of Buddhism back to God, that he is to be born on a body of water where horses graze upon the shores, and where the fields are green. He is an Occidental who shall not sit in the lotus position, but will occupy a straight chair and put his feet on the floor. Many have claimed they were the present world Messiah, but proof is not in evidence. The deliverance of the universal world message must be an age-old teaching.

123

ECK is a complete body of Supreme Wisdom which has silently been waiting for its rediscovery and few have ever had the ability or the courage to confront it. Many of the well-known masters who have disguised themselves as leaders in different fields of religious and philosophical thought have tried to resurrect ECK in the form of a mystery school. They failed mainly because the people of their times were not ready for it.

We have had the same problem throughout the annals of world religious history. If one religion had grown stronger among the political figures and governments, then ECK had to remain underground because of the problems of persecution. Today it has again appeared on the world scene and is somewhat ignored and persecuted because the leaders in various fields of religion, politics and government do not want to see it spread. They fear lest it upset the religious economic balance of the world's nations.

Leaders like myself at the head of the present-age ECK movement have all had the same problem as anyone who has established the true teachings. We are all put in the position of people approaching us wanting anything but God in their lives. This is the primary problem of life. Even Christ had to contend with this. People simply do not recognize these individuals as being Godmen, the agents of the SUGMAD, the Supreme Being manifested in flesh. In other words, they think in terms of what can be done for themselves; the crippled, unhappy, the prisoners of the negative power, disillusioned with life, and without any source of income, wearily make their way to the feet of the gods, magicians, metaphysicians, and other wonder-workers hoping for the miracle cure.

The Godmen who are actually the ECK Masters can do any miracle they desire, but seldom will because it makes the witness believe in physical and psychic phenomena instead of following the true path to God.

The true seekers of miraculous help find sooner or later that real spiritual assistance depends on their inner growth. The more that one is in the higher stages of development, the easier it is for any master to heal him or give him some spiritual help. But those who are still in the nonsurvival stage never can find that miracle for which they seek throughout their lives.

Instead, when reaching the Godman they in desperation ask that he give them something to heal them, fill their empty purses and bring them material happiness. But the Godman gently reminds them that all he has to offer is a way to the Supreme Being, and what they want is not for him to give. Most of them turn away sadly and keep seeking in hopes of finding that miracle which will be a cure-all.

The Godman always does his miracles in silence, when few, if any, are watching. The healing which is demanded of him by many comes so quietly and mysteriously that those who are receiving it hardly recognize it until later. It was my privilege to sit in the company of Sudar Singh, the great ECK Master, years ago when a man asked to be healed of arthritis in his feet. The Master merely smiled and talked about something else while the man impatiently insisted on being healed. Finally he gave up and left, but the limping gait he had when entering the ashram was gone. He now walked like a man without suffering or pain in his feet. His gait was that of a healthy person.

The Godman has but one purpose in being here — to take those who desire back to their heavenly home again. This world is one of wars, pestilence and malignancy which is the training ground for Soul. When each is ready the true master appears and prepares him by special training to make the ascent into the higher worlds by learning to leave this state of physical consciousness while living in the body, and to dwell in the higher worlds. Every day the chela will spend time with the Godman in these higher realms, exploring them and learning what eternity is, and how he will spend his life in it.

Unless one is able to find the true master in this life he will spend more lives in future incarnations perfecting himself until he reaches the state where the path of ECK is opened for him to travel into the heavenly worlds.

125

THE MODERN EMPHASIS ON WORD "SOUL"

To be wrapped in the aura of mysticism is a fad these days, and those pseudo-mystics who have tried to capitalize on the supernatural and bring it down to a common level are in for a real psychic shocker.

These cultists have made absurdity out of many religions and have created faiths which border on the edge of fantasy. Even Madison Avenue has entered into using such words as "Meditation" and "Soul" until they have become as commonplace as the daily words we use describing our feelings about wives, husbands and friends.

Soul should be a word describing that part of man which is divine — the spark of God within man that we know has communication between the Deity and the human consciousness. But the singers, rock and rollers and other entertainers have come up with the use of the word to describe something called "Soul Music", "Soul Food" and other things which are only for the emotional and physical senses.

The entertainment industry is mainly responsible for entering into the field of mysticism. The Beatles were largely to blame for hitching themselves to the star of Indian mysticism — as near as they got to it. They rubbed against a so-called holy man of India and then for some unknown reason proclaimed to possess the whole gamut of divine knowledge and to be able to wear the cloak of divinity.

These people are unable to understand that in opening the door to the psychic worlds they will encounter invisible dangers that can bring to them detrimental changes. The psychic influences they stir up are certainly not at all good for those who are within their reach, be it by remote range or direct contact.

Everybody is defining Soul these days. Ask any entertainer who deals in what is called "Soul Music" and his answer will be, "Soul is what one feels internally. Soul is the blues, hard times, tradition, and the trouble side of life."

126

All that is being said here is that "feeling" is "Soul" to most people. This is hardly anything more than the psychic element of life or what we know as emotion. Emotion is generated from the second plane of life, known in the esoteric language as the astral world. Of what particular use is it when it generally misleads those who are exposed to its influences through music, dialogue and physical contact?

This certainly has nothing to do with the actual spiritual nature of man no matter how much the psuedo-mystics keep trying to tell us otherwise. The magicians in ancient times were well aware of the impact of certain rhythmic beats upon the masses. For example, the bonging of drums in a steady beat hits upon certain psychic centers in the human mind and brings about moral erosion, arouses sensuality and creates corruption of the individual, community and eventually the nation.

A good example is what has happened to those leaders in the world of entertainment and the movie industry who believed they could flaunt the laws of the psychic world and have their own normality. Now many well-known figures have become drug addicts, neurotics, paranoids and even schizophrenics who need to be under medical care instead of performing on stage, screen and television. Such people can influence those who are looking for an idol to worship — usual in any mass society. The hero is taken from any element of life regardless of whether he is a warrior or a rock and roll musician.

The term "Soul", as a mystic or religionist definition, has an altogether different connotation. It means "spiritual awareness" — developing the perception of knowing and seeing or spiritual unfoldment — the attainment of true spiritual insight. One sees and knows through the divine senses within.

I can truthfully say that few, if any, can give a definition of "Soul". But at the same time for Tin-Pan Alley, Madison Avenue and the opportunists to seize upon the very word

127

which to the religionists denotes sacred spiritual meaning, is stepping upon the toes of sacrilege.

It is hypocritical and without foundation for true devotion to label anything commercial with such sacred words as "Soul" and other terms which we have traditionally used for the uplifting of the individual to higher worship and thinking.

AN UNDERSTANDING OF ECKANKAR

The whole purpose of ECKANKAR, the science of Soul Travel, is simply that the individual establishes the fact of survival beyond this life and the management of it.

By the survival of his individual self, he becomes a co-worker with God and is able to manage himself in a modus operandi that brings about an ability to travel in the spiritual worlds on his own strength, will, and choice of directions.

There is an ancient saying, *"Reality is One; sages call it by various names."* Reality is then, of course, a fact. The fact is man can leave his body at his own volition and travel anywhere in the spiritual universes, when and where he desires, while still occupying the physical body.

In their attitude of this there are two groups at opposite extremes — those who have complete faith in Soul Travel and understand survival, and those who do not believe in it and put their faith in the intellectual realm and the senses. The latter group has no concept of survival. They believe vaguely that somehow they will be taken care of after passing from this physical life.

There is hardly a middle stand on this philosophy. Most people will be in one or the other group, arguing for or against the one in which they are not a member. This is generally not a mild argument, but of such force that we are often reminded of the primitives who take up the sword to convert their fellowmen.

With the above in mind, I am going to lay down the principles and the foundation of Soul Travel so that you may have points on which to stand your ground when brought into the position of having to defend your own belief in it.

This will give you the basis for ECK, the Illuminated Way for getting out-of-the-body state of consciousness, which will be taken up later.

The principle of Soul travel is concerned with its purpose — that of establishing survival for one's own self beyond the physical senses. The next step is the management of that survival through our ability to get out of the body state of consciousness. This is the development of a latent talent shared by all persons, a state at which they will arrive sooner or later, whether they believe in it or not.

We have many authentic cases of those who have returned in the spirit form — friends or near relations — who, while in the physical state argued bitterly against Soul Travel. Now they admit they were wrong, that it is possible, and that we must learn it quickly before dropping the physical body forever.

There are very many cases on record of those who were or are able to do this type of projection, e.g., Swedenborg, who founded a church on his experiments and findings. However, the problem has been that so few are able to demonstrate or show anyone else how to do Soul Travel because of lack of knowledge of the principles in this field of phenomena and because of a lack of communication or, in many cases, a difference in semantics.

First, Soul, or self (sometimes called the Tuza by the spiritual travelers or masters) is an individual entity with the ability to function in the fields of magnetized universes.

Second, Soul itself acts by wave lengths and vibratory actinics (the action of sound rays).

Third, Soul has a full range of perception (that is, vision, hearing, smell, etc.) similar to the physical senses but at a higher vibration.

Fourth, all the esoteric bodies — that is, the astral, causal, and mental can be aberrated just the same as the physical self can be.

Fifth, Soul is able to know and understand all things, and is able to function as an independent entity, yet as a co-worker with God, and at the same time dwell in Total Awareness.

These five principles are the ones which we most need to know, although there are another half dozen or so that are really off-shoots from them.

One other principle demands immediate attention:

No two things can occupy the same space in the lower worlds at the same time, except Soul. Two Souls CAN occupy the same space, and this is why it is said that when a man and woman are compatible with one another, living in harmony in the married state, they are as one. Both Souls are occupying the same space.

However, when an individual is dwelling in the spiritual state, he can be one with all things. Here we find that spirit is the actual foundation for all life and that in this state all things can occupy the same space at all times. The law for the lower world does not apply in the higher world.

A brief explanation of these principles is that Soul is actually an individual entity which has freedom to do as it wishes. However, its true purpose is to give service to its maker and to help those who wish to return to their heavenly home.

Soul has the ability of motion, movement and action throughout the universes by its own volition, thus freedom to travel in any universe within itself. God gave such gifts to Soul because IT wanted Soul to return eventually to its own abode in the highest spiritual realm — that which we know as the Ocean of Love and Mercy. This is one of the spiritual gifts which St. Paul speaks of in the 12th chapter of First Corinthians; healing, prophecy and wisdom are also among these gifts. In the Christian Bible the light body is that in which we travel until reaching the fifth or Soul plane where Soul enters into its pure state. This pure state often is called the Glorious body.

Soul is therefore able to move or have action by the use of vibratory actinics, or what is known to the physical senses as the action of sound and light rays.

I will not discuss the sound current until later, but at present will dwell on the sound rays. These, as anyone who has been well grounded in spiritual studies will know, are vibrations coming out of the highest heavens downward into the physical world. We often call them cosmic rays, especially when they are the light rays. This the energy which Soul uses to travel in the other worlds. It is not really a complicated affair as many believe, but a form of energy used in the same manner that we gather energy from plants, minerals and animal life for our action in this universe.

The difference is that as travelers in the spiritual worlds we use thought energy, a form of cosmic energy, for movement up to the fifth plane. We then transfer again to a higher form of energy for Total Awareness.

To simplify: we use this energy, thought energy, to move in and out of the body by shifting of attention from body consciousness to thought consciousness. Soul is, in a sense, the consciousness of the whole self — an awareness of viewpoint. Once we have this awareness under control we can fix our attention anywhere we desire and can move it to any plane we wish. Hence, Soul Travel. We can thus be seen in the form in which others know us at any other place, at any distance from where we are fixed physically. In the same manner we can travel in the universes — invisible to most people — where we all go after leaving this world.

The very simplicity of this makes Soul traveling complicated for most of us.

Soul is able to perceive through Its own senses outside the body. I am not speaking of the psychic senses, but of the spiritual senses which perceive beauty far more readily than our physical or astral senses. This is the reason why so many mystics, saints, holy men and travelers who are able to receive the cosmic consciousness, and those who can travel in the spiritual universes are often beautified with such shining countenances and eyes. This is what enables them to speak of the wondrous worlds beyond. The light and sound beyond fills all space with such beauty that we who remain limited by our physical senses have little knowledge of and can never experience it.

Soul also has an ability to cognize. This is the act of knowing coupled with awareness and judgment. It is the grasping of knowledge by the faculty of awareness, which is passed on to the body senses for action. Soul knows instantly

132

what is to be known to Itself. It finds that the scale of ability ascends in this fashion: Seeing, Knowing, Being.

Soul's sheaths or coverings as we know them — the physical, astral, causal, mental and other bodies — can be aberrated in the same manner as the physical self. We find people with psychic aberrations as well as those with astral or mental problems. Sudar Singh, whom I speak of often as the Master who introduced me to ECKANKAR, traveled occasionally to India to help those who were called Masts. These are people who are half in the body and half out, a psychic condition originating on the astral plane and causing abnormal behavior. Usually this is not violent behavior, but of an unusual pattern — for example, accepting a pet as the reincarnation of a deceased mate, or sweeping the sidewalk daily with a handbroom.

Sudar Singh would put these people, called Masts, back into their bodies or get them out so they would have relief from these psychic phenomena. They were people whom we in the western world would consider to be neurotic or psychotic enough to be confined in mental hospitals.

Soul is able to know and understand all things by being, knowing and viewing. It has this faculty within itself. It is able to act as part of the whole of God's worlds, and yet at the same time to perform as an independent entity, a co-worker with the Supreme, where it can dwell in the Cosmic Consciousness.

It can do all things outside the body, but within the body, of itself, it is limited. Outside it will have a 360-degree perimeter vision.

The basic principle of ECK, the ancient science of Total Awareness, is that the lower worlds of creation are finished and that the origin of all creation in these worlds below the fifth plane lies within each of us.

Therefore, the way by which each person can regain the original mastership of his own spiritual Garden of Eden is by use of the spiritual eye, called the Ajna, or Tisra Til. The Supreme Deity has endowed each of us with this faculty as

133

the divine way to reach the inner worlds beyond the physical senses.

ECKANKAR teaches us that we can have solace in Nirvikalpa, that form of deep samadhi in which the participant cannot distinguish himself from the object of his participation, a state of oneness with the divine spirit. Such Soul Travel experiences in awareness were common in the lives of the old Christian saints and Eastern adepts.

A variation of the system of ECK is taught today. It is called Shabda Yoga, the yoga of sound current, but the system is known as Santon Ki Shiksha, the yoga of the audible life stream. It is sometimes known as Ananda Yoga — the yoga of happiness and bliss. But as said, it is only an offshoot, or a splinter group, formed out of ECK.

All human hope and effort centers about three things in the precepts of ECK. They are (1) Self-Realization (2) God-Realization and, (3) entering into the Kingdom of Heaven, either in this life or in the next.

To practice Soul Travel out of curiosity in search of new sensations or in or in order to gain psychic powers is a mistake which is finished with futility, neurosis or even worse.

To practice it while studying or practicing another system, or even trying to mix it with another path, almost invariably brings problems to the practitioner.

None should seek to develop his latent talent for Soul Travel without knowing that he must practice discipline in order to reach the point where he progressively learns the value of renunciation of perishable things, and finds that even in success and worldly happiness he is really an exile in this world and must some day start the journey toward the upper regions.

The whole purpose of ECK is to give us an understanding of spiritual liberation within this lifetime. It is to show us there is salvation in this life, or survival of the true self. No other system is so oriented except the Hindu religious teachings — Vedanta, Yoga, etc. — which can give us a sense of immortality, but not a proof of survival.

There is no need waiting until death to gain complete liberation and freedom. It can be accomplished simply through Soul Travel. Since it is as individual an experience as birth, living and dying, we must come to a realization of it within ourselves, and not through anyone else. It is a question of surrendering one's self to the Other Self, or surrendering one's self to that which is within us, the spark of God or whatever we wish to call it. Many look upon it as the Inner Master, or the liberator. It is this Self which will become the dominant aspect of Soul and can guide it in and out of the body consciousness.

The spiritual masters all teach that there is no means of spiritual liberation except through Soul Travel. Without actual conscious participation in this art of freedom, no one can ever get out of this life with liberation and escape any reincarnation and karma.

The mind control system has failed us because it is a fact of history that not one man has ever learned to control his organs of sense by the power of his own mind, simply by willing it so. Will power may hold impulses and desires in check, but if one is to overcome completely his desires and impulses, he must find something which the mind likes better. It can never be accomplished by negation alone.

Therefore, will power is not the key to Soul Travel. Imagination is the faculty that we use in getting in and out of the body, for in the conflict between will power and imagination, it is always the latter that wins.

Did you ever hear of the Law of Reversed Effort?

Here is an example of it. If one walks across a plank between two chairs about five feet high, there is no problem; but if the planks are raised to one hundred feet in height, then we struggle with the imagination which conjures up all sorts of fears of the body falling.

What I am trying to say here is that Soul Travel is controlled by the imaginative process within the first three planes, and thereafter by the reality of spiritual effort. For example, one evening while sitting in silence doing the spiritual exercises of ECK, I, Soul, popped out of the body

135

high into space. I was looking down on what might have been a jungle area, as though from an airplane. The action of Soul getting out of the body was so swift that my heart jumped in anxiety at being so high without any support. Instantly It, Soul, hopped back into the body for security. It took several minutes of coaxing to control the imagination and get back out again.

The imagination is not what the psychologists dwell upon. The Law of Reversed Effort is that the imagination functions by negation, for we are drawn into that which we are trying to avoid. This faculty of imagination is that which William Blake, the seventeenth century poet, wrote about. It is indeed interesting for it is only a picture machine running off reels inside the mind for Soul to observe.

There is nothing it can show which is not reality somewhere in the spiritual universes. These are pictures taken by Soul in Its many flights, and the ability to keep them for playbacks when drawn upon. We think we are conjuring them up as an image, as an original, an archetype, but this is not true.

Everything we think of, or imagine, exists in the other worlds. All planes up to the fourth are exactly like this world, except that they exist in finer vibrations than this plane. The physical universe is the coarsest of all planes.

We should take control over the negation of imagination; that is, keep clear the images of what we wish to do, instead of letting those which are concerned with failure take over. This can be called the adoption of an attitude. What we are in is a state of consciousness, for everything is a state of consciousness. Once we learn this, Soul Travel becomes as natural as the functions of eating and sleeping.

Remember that Christ said, "I go to prepare a place for you in my Father's house!" He meant that where the subtle body goes the others must follow. For example, if we place the imagination somewhere, the rest of the Self must follow. If we place it in the astral plane we must certainly follow there, for either a permanent or temporary stay. This is a spiritual law, for all things must follow the Law of Image, not

136

thought — for thought cannot bring results. Again Christ said: "Take no thought for you cannot add one cubit to your stature."

If many believe leaving the body to be a hardship, that is because they wish to remain inside the body, for there is a certain security about being in this temple of flesh. Those who understand the spiritual exercises, or methods of Soul Travel, know the means and ways of keeping the spirit imprisoned in the body or exiled outside it.

Napoleon and Alexander the Great, greatest conquerors in the history of the West, were able to do Soul Travel in order to watch the progress of the battles they fought and won. It is said that Alexander stood outside his body while winning his three greatest victories — Gaugamela, Issus, Hyaspes — and was able to direct his troops to victory because of his greater view of the battlefields.

Napoleon often played cards with his staff officers while the battle was in progress, but he was only keeping his body busy while he surveyed the field. This was particularly true at his greatest victory, at Austerlitz, on December 2, 1805.

The results of Soul Travel often are successful in many fields. It's said that Arthur Stockwell, great financier in the 19th century, was able to do Soul Travel and thereby received information needed for his financial promotions.

Longevity and health are the best indications of this phenomenon, and a knowingness that does not come with intellectual awareness, but only with spiritual insight.

Above all is the ECK Marg, the path to the Supreme SUGMAD, and those who follow it eventually will find their way into the heavenly worlds again.

SITUATION THIRTY

Situation Thirty is a coined expression which designates a spiritual, mental or physical crisis for anyone.

The phrase is well-known among those who are the followers of ECKANKAR, the ancient science of Soul Travel.

Since we are seeking God refuge, that state of living in God, it is not out of place to point out that ECKANKAR is a path to the Ultimate Heavenly Realm.

It is a unique path but nevertheless one which has been used since the dawn of time in this universe by the saints, masters and saviours passed on via oral instruction until this present Aquarian age.

Without doubt it is a panacea for Situation Thirty in the areas of troubles, woes and illness of the human state of consciousness that assaults man in his present state.

ECKANKAR is a depth spiritual psychology that digs into the nature of man. Going beyond the mental realm we are able to explore the worlds where the roots of man's troubles are created as causes and leave us with the effects of irrational outer behavior.

The human race has been brought to a state of Situation Thirty because of a lack of individual awareness. This awareness should bring us into the natural state of man called God-Awareness.

We are being taught today to live collectively, that all are responsible for one another, especially our brother's welfare and behavior in this world. This is not true. We are seekers of God; we are to develop self-responsibility and be the sole responsible one for our own welfare and behavior in this world. This is individualism. Unless we accept this responsibility for ourselves, then our efforts have been wasted. God does not want anyone who is not able to make his own way through the worlds into His kingdom.

Because of this we must therefore learn that to become greater in the Kingdom of Heaven is to take self-responsibility. Experience in life will teach us such goals are necessary in order to survive.

This survival means that we are going into the spiritual worlds as ones who are strong in spirit and in what is called here character. Good character is only that which brings goodness into our lives. It is like saying that good karma results in God's mercy and love.

The world's nations are in the position of Situation Thirty as well as the individual whose problems and woes are sinking him into a deep morass.

Unless he turns to God it will be a long time before he will be able to get himself into the right path to reach the heavenly worlds.

It might be a long time before he finds ECKANKAR and total consciousness.

KARMA AND REINCARNATION

The most basic understanding in the study of ECKANKAR, the ancient science of Soul Travel, is that man is Soul living in a physical body in order to function in the physical universe. Soul cannot "die", but bodies can. Soul goes from body to body in what we call lives. Soul has been sent by Its creator, GOD, to the lower worlds to gain experiences. This is done by Soul through many lifetimes, and when It reaches a certain point of experiencing It returns home to Its creator. Thus GOD becomes aware of the experiences of the many, many lifetimes lived by Soul and the spiritual wisdom and power gained through them. We call this returning of Soul again and again to experience in the lower worlds of matter energy, space, and time reincarnation.

While Soul is dwelling in the lower worlds, It is subjected to an exact payment for everything that is done. This is what we call karma. In every experience, be it painful or otherwise, there is a compensation power to be gained or a reward which is well worth the suffering necessary to build it into Soul-growth. This is the great law of the lower worlds, but not that of the real Kingdom of Heaven. The laws of karma and reincarnation exist in the lower worlds simply for the purpose that the effect of our cause bring to Soul the opportunity to learn certain lessons which It has not learned in previous lives.

Soul exists simply because of GOD'S love for It, and It exists eternally. This is the law of love that brings Soul through all Its experiences so that it may gain Soul-quality for further progress back to God Worlds where It then becomes free of the laws of karma and reincarnation.

I'M A CLIFF HANGER
AND I LIKE IT!

I've always been an authentic individualist!

First indications of my fierce hatred of restrictions came about at age three when I hammered out a windowpane with my tiny but bloody fists in protest of being locked in.

My half-sister gave me the nonce "Cliff Hanger" then, and it stuck. It's an old gypsy slang tag for one who bursts all barriers to get to the top of the cliff where he can be free from the crowd below.

When the late Jerry Wald made an oblique offer of a significant amount of money for movie rights on my book, "Shadows of Destiny", I turned thumbs down. Later I let TransCon Films of England pick up an option of it for far less than the original amount.

So far it hasn't been near filming, but I don't care. When I learned that I'd have no voice in the screen treatment of my book if bought by an American film company, my reactions were to hell with it. It was for that reason I took a chance and turned down any U.S. offer that came my way and let a European company have it even on option.

I just happened to be sentimental about that story. Besides money isn't everything; freedom and independence even about my work are just as important.

Everybody who knew something about this episode shook their skull boxes and muttered, "That proves Paul Twitchell is independent!"

It might sound crazy, but I'm just that independent, and will tell anyone to stick his head in the lake. It's happened many times. For instance, at the Seattle Post Intelligencer where I worked briefly in 1961, when told to stop wearing my crazy caps to work, I reacted in the usual independent way and said, "I'll wear my caps anywhere I wish, including

141

the P.I. office!" Under usual circumstances I would have been fired then, but lucky for me the bookkeeping department made a mistake in my paycheck to the tune of $325 overpayment. I held on to it until everybody saw things my way and after returning the money quietly resigned.

Another occasion when working for a small weekly newspaper, the publisher wanted to fire me for some reason or other, but I had the only key to the door in my pocket and refused to quit. He had to hire me back again to get his key, but only on the promise to keep me on the job.

Restrictions smother me. They make me restless and unable to stay very long in one place. That's why I have lived in so many places here and abroad.

I've never gotten involved in the comic game of politics. It's never interested me to vote, and when the Johnson versus Goldwater campaigns got underway I steered completely as far out as possible from any involvement.

Who wants to get tangled up with politics? I certainly don't. It means getting tangled up with the politicians and clergy which are supported and cared for by our society to the tune of our own money by taxation. They all believe in the old maxim, "Don't do as I do, but do as I say." It's all tied in with suburbia, mass culture, and is an insult to the American people.

I'm a lone wolf. I live in solitude as much as possible. I hardly ever look at television, listen to the radio, and keep away from newspapers. I live indifferently to any political or religious philosophy and this mass society because of its many social ills which not even God could cure if He were interested.

I'm not a restriction smasher. Nothing in religion can make me climb a wall. I'm not interested in proclaiming a great love for children, raising money for hospitals, or joining any cause which has a noble purpose.

Among my revolts against the great society is my approval sticker, "Recommended by Paul Twitchell", with my own face on it. It's sort of a spoof at the Good Housekeeping Seal of Approval, the AAA approvals, Diner Cards, Duncan Hines,

142

Betty Crocker, Prudence Penny and Ann Landers.

Some people take this Seal of Approval seriously. It was used as a promotional piece on candy wrappers for the Newall Confectionary Company, Montreal, the Maryland Motor Bike Co., Baltimore, a Seattle men's clothing store, and was sold in most college book stores across the country as a comic sticker. I even drew a royalty off its distribution and sales.

I've distributed the Seal of Approval to dozens of celebrities, e.g., Ed Sullivan, Eleanor Roosevelt, Roy Crane, Jim Bishop, Al Capp, Jack Benny and Ian Fleming, to name a few. Their reaction was one of amusement — which was the only way to take it.

But my other award, "Paul Twitchell Sour Grapes Award," has upset people who received it. It went to William Drury, daily columnist, News Call-Bulletin, San Francisco, for a dreary column he wrote on speed reading.

He retaliated with a blistering attack on me personally in his daily column. The paper offered free space for a reply. Results were that some business houses learned about my approval sticker and requested use of it for promotion pieces for their products.

Ed Sullivan's reaction was delightful. He remarked, "I'm delighted and amazed!" But the effects of the Sour Grapes Award has been either caustic or complete silence. Hugh Hefner, Playboy's publisher, got one for his effeminate philosophy, but it came back without comment. When I ribbed Cavalier with it, Fred Birmingham, the editor, sent it back with a light tongue-in-cheek note.

I intended to send it to Frank Sinatra for his turkey, "Robin and the Seven Hoods," President Johnson for his Great Society kick, John O'Hara for his book, "Elizabeth Appleton," Justice William Douglas for his liberalism, Owen Spann, KGO radio, San Francisco for his program, and James Farmer for his gentle approach to solving our civil rights problem (he only wants to tear the legs off tables if he can't eat with other people).

These awards have been left in thousands of books as

143

markers in public libraries over the country. I've had letters, telephone calls and personal visits from people who agreed with me or wanted to break my leg for speaking out because they did not understand these were only book markers.

The path of ECKANKAR, which resulted out of my works published in European journals, has gained a wide following throughout the world. ECKANKAR was formed out of my own experiences with out-of-the-body travel.

I never smoke. If I can't drink champagne, I won't drink at all. I write several hours a night, skip-read several thousand books a year, travel constantly, and shun a safe existence on the assembly line of our soap opera society. I've seventy-five sport caps and hats, and drive small foreign cars.

I'm against the flapdoodles of these times, e.g., togetherness, credit cards, insurance, and our supermarket culture which puts so much emphasis on the so-called aid to better living. I dislike career women and student political groups grubbing for money because they represent a society that trespasses on my independence and freedom.

After I withdrew from a Yoga retreat in 1955, I went off to India for a spell. Following this I settled in England to write another book, but the death of my half-sister brought me home.

Roaming around without purpose I landed in Seattle where I met Gail, a twenty-year-old University of Washington coed whom I later married. A year later incidents occurring out of a column I was doing for a weekly newspaper, including a black eye, because of an unfortunate piece of copy done just prior to the Dallas tragedy, got me on the road again.

From the day I knocked the windowpane out of the door I've been a Cliff Hanger and liked it, for it gives me freedom and independence to do as I please.

NEWS SPLINTERS
IN OUR SOCIAL ORDER

The splinters which began to show in our social order following World War I were evident by the era which Scott Fitzgerald called the Lost Generation.

We have succeeded in this country most successfully with a few others, mainly the jazz age, the flapper era, and the beatniks, while England has been visited by the angry young men and the Outsiders, all showing that something is amiss in western civilization.

For this reason when interviewed last year by one of the leading Hearst newspapers in Seattle, Washington, I discussed at length my own thinking about these times. I coined the name of my attitude "The Cliff Hanger."

Immediately I was besieged by telephone calls and mail asking, "What in heaven's name was a Cliff Hanger?" So heavy were the requests that I abandoned all hope of ever getting across my idea to the public that it was a tag merely to explain my attitude regarding this age of mass culture as a lot of abracadabra.

The name is synonymous of a man hanging on the edge of a cliff, safe from the crowd, more outside than the outsider, happier than the angry young men, and at the opposite pole from the Existentialist who claims man has no hope in life.

The ways of this homogeneous civilization has left the Cliff Hanger with no alternative than to turn his back on our square-headed society and go his way with those who might have been called Cliff Hangers ere before his time, e.g., Lord Byron, Tom Paine, Rimbaud, Lawrence of Arabia, and others who have earned the various tags of non-conformist, individualist, rebel and lonely oddballs.

No Cliff Hanger is interested in public bangles, nor willing to give himself the airs of a hero by proclaiming a great love

145

to raise money for hospitals or worthy causes which involve the enthusiasm of the middle classes. Neither is there anything in this mass age great enough to make him climb a wall, especially in religion.

This zany character's attitude of mind might be called the vanguard of a new religious thought. At least after I surfaced a different mystic belief called ECKANKAR, a Pali word for co-worker with God, did a lot of people start corresponding with me. This unorthodox philosophy received wide welcome among the European intellectual and college circles that followed the publication of my works in foreign magazines.

The Cliff Hanger doesn't use drugs of any kind, only the natural mystic methods. He seeks solace in meditation and bilocation experiences common in the lives of the old Christian savants. His saints are Kabir, 16th century Hindu poet/weaver, the ancient Sufi avatars Jala al-din Rumi, Hafi and Shamus-i-Tabiz, and Rebazar Tarzs of Lhasa, Tibet.

History is made by the impact of the eccentrics, the originals, the proud imaginative people from whom new ideas flow. A society cannot get along without its Cliff Hangers because they are the most vivid means of exhibiting the power of free men.

For the same reason this break is necessary with our mass culture because it has considered the man of imagination and free spirit dangerous. He is an incarnation of ideals in men, from the spirit of Socrates and the imagination of Blake to the compassion of Buddha and the freedom of Cyrano de Bergerac.

He is the man who should have an I.Q. of 185 on the Benet scale and can skip-read four to six thousand books a year. He generally makes his living in one of the aesthetic arts, out to have his own lingo for communication, and has earned the label of illogic in philosophy and deed.

He should be able to reject the great unwashed who are up to their ears in this department store of culture, of pension plans, telephones, radios and TV, dogma and money changers.

146

Accordingly, I see this civilization heading down the path to destruction, and the Cliff Hanger will be the greatest to suffer unless he can get out of it quickly. But he is in a sense like Thoreau who wasn't in the least interested in changing the ways of his time, but wants to be left alone to enjoy his own company in solitude.

His works and deeds are always pointed toward this, although they may appear on the surface like the efforts of a man careless of law and landlords with the attitude of gay mockery.

The Cliff Hanger may be the favorite of the Gods, and it's certain he is the lonely hero of his times. But, as I said before, his appearance in any civilization shows the splintering of the social order.

ECK AND MUSIC

Few people hardly think of ECK and music simultaneously, but the very fact that the Sound Current, the audible life current, is the origin of all melodies in the universes of the world makes it a spiritual truth.

The ECK is the fundamental principle in the spiritual works. In fact it might be said that IT is the supreme factor of the universe of the worlds of God.

IT is the Voice of God. Whenever IT speaks or acts there is sound and it may be heard by the spiritual ears of man. This divine current or wave which is called the ECK goes forth from the SUGMAD and flows through all eternity, touching all life; IT sustains life and gives man hope for eternal existence.

When SUGMAD speaks, everything in existence vibrates and this creates the ECK, the divine sound, and IT can be heard by the spiritual ears which have been trained to hear IT. This is the way in which the Supreme Deity can be heard and seen. IT is a luminous and musical wave.

With the trained musician the ECK is transposed from the inner to the outer senses and a new composition is brought to the world. Great musicians like Beethoven, Mozart, and Chopin had this ability to translate the music of the spheres into a physical sound for the public.

When listening, too many of the music masters of this plane will not hear the outpouring of the vital and lyrical impulses from the inner worlds. Some, however, will be swept away by sheer musical ecstasy and get the feeling that the music is bubbling up from the heart of the composer with the spontaneity of a bird in the spring morning sunlight.

The listener to any music should aim for multiplying all possible sources of enjoyment instead of trying to hear the Voice of God singing through the heart and mind of the composer. It will not become realty to him until this is established within himself as a part of his own being. Once he starts listening to the music of the classic composers with a sense of ecstasy then he begins to unfold spiritually. This is part of the spiritual law. He must learn to listen with the inner ears, and not with the mind.

Good music will help in the spiritual unfoldment of the chela by gaining self-knowledge. This level of consciousness is known to man as Self-Realization, the consciousness of one's own self in the Soul state. It is a gradual process of lifting the self, or rather unfolding spiritually until reaching this particular level of attainment.

The divine ECK, the sound or word, stands for all that God is or has ever been or done. It includes all ITS qualities and is the only way that God can manifest ITSELF to the human consciousness.

I strongly emphasize that self-knowledge can be gained through music. This is borne out by the fact that the ancient mysteries had varied programs of music to accompany their initiations and for their secret meetings. This was especially true for the mystery religions of ancient Greece whose origins were purely nature worship. The followers tried to imitate nature with their musical instruments and in the dance. The woodwinds were largely derived from a basic musical instrument which when played would raise the spiritual level of the followers at meetings by imitating the sounds of nature. These sounds would be in essence an imitation of nature's sounds, e.g., the wind, waves, and birds calling, to name a few.

The sounds of ECK are different on various planes; for example, in studying these harmonies we find they are developed through ten aspects of the body of man. They are: the sound of running water; the roaring of the ocean; the jingling of bells; the running water of a brook; the buzzing of bees; the twittering of sparrows; the music of violins; the whistle and then the flute, and finally that which becomes the HU, the most sacred of all sounds.

The HU is the sacred name for God. It is, or has been, the

secret name until this time when it is supposed to become public. It is the beginning and ending of all sounds, whether they are from man, beast or creature.

The SUGMAD, God, is known to the mystics of the Vairagi Order as the HU. It is the only name possible to give to this Supreme Deity. It is the only name in which all sound can be proclaimed. Therefore it is found in every piece of music that we hear from Rock and Roll to the most Classical and Sacred. It is the background of all words and sounds. The very spirit which underlies the words and sounds and is hidden under them all, as well as the body of man, is the divine ECK.

The divine sound current will bring one who practices the spiritual exercises of ECKANKAR a release from the dense form of existence. It will lift the practitioner into those higher worlds where he can gain God knowledge. This is the music of the spheres, the divine voice of the SUGMAD which gives the chela that knowledge of the worlds beyond the physical universe.

What we are doing here is raising ourselves into the other worlds and visiting the planes where the higher spiritual entities live and get a renewed outlook on the whole of life. While dwelling in the human consciousness we are too much the slaves of our moods and emotions.

The chela never uses music as an escape but for the very purpose of lifting himself above the human consciousness. He knows that every group that uses music will have an entity or angel that takes charge and inspires those who are the audience. For example, a military parade with all its stirring music attracts an angel, one which is the guardian of military music and is used as a vehicle for the higher forces to pour energies into the listeners.

This is true also of the individual who turns on the radio or puts a record on the phonograph. What the quality of music is will be that which attracts the quality of the entity to be with him. If it is rock and roll he will pull to himself those entities which draw the lowest form of beings. These will pour forces from the lower astral plane into the Indri chakra

150

which will stir the sexual forces and create a disturbance in the listeners.

The beat of rock and roll reacts upon the Indri chakra. The steady beat of lower chords of music is similar to that of the drums. The latter were used by the priests in the ancient times to stir people emotionally and create sex orgies. By the use of the type of music they could control the public. It is hardly anything other than black magic, done deliberately to get a hold upon people, especially the young. This is evident today.

This is the work of the Kal forces for music, more than anything else, can either break up or establish a social order of a nation, or groups of nations. For example, the pattern of thought can be established through any type of music. The aura of the individual, which can be seen by any good clairvoyant, will show the aberrations and patterns of thought established by whatever type of music the person had during his early years, like that which might be popular at the time throughout a nation, for it certainly influences the inner bodies of man. It is the reason why certain sections of the various countries, e.g., the Ozark mountains, the deep South, or the Wales of England, and the Transylvania mountains, as well as the region of Georgia in Russia, to name a few, are vastly different from other parts of their respective nations. The music created by the folklore and by home talent often fixes the auras of the people of these regions so they are forced to think differently from the other natives. Every country in the world has its own sectionism with which it must contend as almost a different nation, apart from its own government.

Tin Pan Alley was the cause of the breakup of the mold of the established thought pattern in the world youth during the early part of this century. The Victorian age had created a fixed, rigid sort of thought pattern which caused most countries in the English speaking world, and those under the British flag, to live by a code of life we called the Protestant Code.

This was all created by the music of the great composer

151

George Frederick Handel, the German born English musician, who became the state musician under Queen Victoria of England. Fortunately, one hardly hears his music played today. He was a ponderous, heavy composer whose works seemed to oppress and regiment the people instead of giving liberation through something more light and gay. His depth of music was gloomy and repressive as most German music composed in the classic style has always been, but Handel's seemed to be more than most.

This created aberrations and heavy fixed patterns of thought within the auras of the peoples of England. As a national idea of life they fell into a mental trap which was to repress them as a nation for almost two centuries. It drew a dark, heavy entity into their orbit and caused disaster to the nation and its empire. Here and there a few brilliant minds gleamed through the heavy mental fog to keep England's name in the foreground of nations, but not too often.

It wasn't until Igor Fedorovich Stravinsky, the Russian born American composer, arrived on the musical scene that the effects of Handel's works began to break up for the good of the world. Rimski-Korsakov and a few others had already started the trend of breaking up the rigid thought patterns. But it took Stravinsky to start the flood in of new ideas and make way for what has become the age of indecency and disharmony. His work, the Rite of Spring, created a disturbance in the musical world in Paris during the year 1912 and a riot in Paris in 1913 and was discontinued and kept off the stage for several years.

It was a shout of defiance against all that was considered the established thought of his day. Whereas the composers up until this time had written and conducted music which was rhythmical and smooth to the world, Stravinsky had created the music of discord and inharmonies. This type of music began to break up the fixed patterns of thought throughout the world. People did not like it because it almost drove them crazy.

In a sense he was like the wild, crazy kids who compose the nerve-wracking rock and roll music today. Its jangling, ear splitting noise strikes the thought patterns so strongly that it is nerve-wracking to those who have listened to sweet syncopating music all their lives, or have been versed in the classics. They simply cannot stand it because it drives them out of their skulls.

Anyone who is set in his ways can be driven wild by listening to two of Stravinsky's works, Petrouchka and Circus and Polka. The disharmony in these pieces of music will start breaking up any set ideas, opinions and habits that one has. When he starts losing these, when they begin to break up in his aura, he feels that something is being lost and it can drive him close to insanity if he cannot mentally grasp something to which he can cling.

The establishment of a new pattern of thinking with the composers of music always causes problems in our social structure. Take, for example, the music of Richard Wagner whose operas, created in the last century, caused an upset to the musical world and hence had its influence on the Hitler regime. Wagner, who was a national socialist, created a new form of opera which demanded a heavy bass voice, and which no one in his day could sing because there was no one trained for this type of opera. He met with failure every time someone produced his works until finally he was forced to build his own opera house at Bayreuth.

The Nazi party leaders, like Hitler and Goering, became so enthralled with Wagner's interpretation of the German superman that they adopted him as the state musician long after Wagner's death. His works, like Tristan and Isolde, Parsifal, and the Ring of the Nibelung, have long withstood the assaults by the staid old forces which never want change.

Others, like Liszt, Berlioz, Beethoven and Paganini, knew the power that music has upon the aura of the audience. Few were aware of what effect discordant music would have on the future generations apparently gloomy over the prospects of the world to come. Wagner tried his best to give the world the basic word of the Sound Current. He had studied under the great ECK Master, Yaubl Sacabi, in the spiritual city of Agam Des. He knew the principles of ECKANKAR and tried to apply them, but it was useless in the face of a world where the ego of the human consciousness holds control over people by the power of the Kal.

When a person who has a good ear for music and who knows the works of ECK listens closely to Wagner's Parsifal and Tannhauser, he will hear clearly the sacred word HU in them. It can also can be heard in his other major works, such as Tristan and Isolde, the Ring of the Nibelung, The Flying Dutchman, Lohengrin, Die Meistersinger, and Siegried.

Moussorgsky's works brought about a similar reaction in Russia during the early part of the last century, especially with his famous work, A Night on Bald Mountain. Mozart's Magic Flute has some of the same tone of the HU, and so does Beethoven's works, as well as Edward MacDowell, the American composer. The list is quite impressive, but one wonders how these composers with such a varied background came to know something about the universal word HU. Somehow or other they came under the direction of an ECK Master who taught them in person or via the dream state.

Many persons do receive instructions and ideas about their work, be it music or literature. If they are this fortunate then it means they have gained liberation, a release from the material environment and given mastership over slavery. It brought about a change in whoever would listen to the inner instruction given by the ECK masters who chose their chelas, knowing that whosoever would listen were to become channels for God to give out the message of the Divine Being. If they did not, then the masters turned their backs on them and sought somewhere else. Many persons have missed their opportunity to serve because they were doubtful of the real message coming through the inner senses.

Others like Liszt, Berlioz, Paganini and Beethoven have been pioneers in new forms of music which served to break up the patterns of the old. These patterns are actually swirling types of aberrations which occupy the aura and create damage to the individual who has allowed himself to be influenced by the types of music which are aberrative, like Handel's.

154

The discordant music can be found in the basic beat of drums, bongos, stringed instruments, and some wind pieces. The heavy beat of drums and electrical guitars are certainly discordant and will almost drive anyone into insanity who listens to it for any time at all, especially if the listener is in close quarters like a cellar room used many times for night clubs. The loudness of the rock and roll beat is damaging not only to the psyche, but to the eardrums, and today we find many old time rock and roll musicians are partially deaf.

This is the work of the Kal power, which we know as the negative, and it can disrupt a whole nation, upset a civilization, and eventually bring about a downfall of the social order unless stopped in the beginning.

In his book "Memories, Dreams and Reflections" Carl Jung, the famous Swiss psychologist, speaks about polyphonic music which he could not abide but was interested in as a study. He found in nature a strange thing occurring, like a teakettle boiling, which sounded like many voices or stringed instruments. This natural melody contained for him all the discords of nature, for, as he said, all nature although harmonious is also contradictory and chaotic. He speaks of being disturbed by listening to a kettle boiling over a fire.

Man becomes upset when he is confronted with chaotic music or what we know as polyphonic music — many sounds in one main stream. He has become enslaved to one way of living, a slave of a fixed habit of nature, and cannot leave this established throught pattern although he may try a dozen different methods or spiritual paths to break this sort of mental aberration which has been implanted in his aura, the magnetic field which surrounds him.

If anyone has an opportunity to listen to Tibetan music he will understand what I am saying here about discordant music. It is likely that Tibetan music is the most discordant type of music in the world. The natives of the little country known as the "Roof of the World" do not know harmonies, although the melodies may be pleasing. At the same time it is pointed out that a Tibetan band can pass easily from the gloomy to the gay and changes of musical rhythm are frequent.

The best of Tibetan music is not found in the large city of Lhasa, which is by far the only one which has any population at all. Some of the capitals of the provinces are simply small villages, so small that we could hardly even call them villages. For example, Gartok, capital of the Western Province of Tibet, has only two houses and some tents. But it is in this sort of place that native music which is discordant is best heard and is that which will break up the patterns of thought.

Most of the Tibetan music of this type is found in the monasteries. The authorities of the spiritual communities know what discordant music and art will do for the individual who is studying and serving in a monastery. The Tibetan art is also patterned along the same idea for breaking up any poor influences on the astral body. This is exactly the point that I am trying to get across here: that music of any nature has an influence on the astral body, if it's the lower plane music. This is certainly one of the traps of the Kal power.

What we are trying to do here is break up the influence of the Kal power which is actually the music of rock and roll, jazz, and pop which has so much discordance in it. This includes pop art and the psychedelic culture which has sprung up during this decade.

The problem with the discordant music and art is that there is nothing to replace the engrams which are pulled out by these two forms of culture. If the individual is under the Living ECK Master then he has no worry, for the Master is taking care of him. The whole failure of the individual in our society is that he is apt to find himself making no spiritual progress without the ECK Master.

ECK is the heart of the consciousness. But the point is that the chela is generally confused because he is trying to absorb too much. He is listening to discordant music, reading and studying other subjects which are not the way of ECKANKAR. When he is doing this there is little chance for him to make any spiritual progress.

156

The problem with ECK is the understanding of it. Some of the words are not familiar to our ear and tongue. It originated out of the Amdo dialect, which is not a basic Tibetan language. The Amdo people are from the area by the same name in China in the province of Chinghai, but its inhabitants are almost all Tibetan.

The Kal music which is spoken about here, not the heavenly which can be heard when one practices the spiritual exercises of ECK, influences the inner bodies of man, especially the astral body. The particular manner in which it grasps the minds of the naive is certainly astounding, and more so in the varied ways that it holds to the feelings and emotions of man, all of which are the mechanics of the astral body. This is the psychic center which is known as the Indri chakra which governs the reproductive organs. It is located near the sacral plexus and is sometimes called the Shat-dal-Kanwal. It has six lotus petals and the color is fiery red. This is the seat also of the astral music and where the entity known to the ECK masters as the Siren of Shat-Dal resides. She is commonly called the Shat-Dal and has the purpose of drawing and holding Soul to the astral world. She is an entity with the shape and face of an extraordinary beautiful woman and a high sweet voice. She is often as wild and fiery as the gowns she wears and has a complexion and hair of a deep reddish color.

The Shat-Dal plays a mandrang, sort of a flutelike instrument which can be found commonly among the Orientals. Whenever rock and roll music plays she appears as the wild, gyrating girl of youthful years. If there is jazz or sweet music she might be a woman of maturity whose dancing seems to be so lovely and graceful.

The Shat-Dal is the daughter of the Kali. This is the entity of the negative world hierarchy whom I have spoken about in the "Flute of God" who has lived on this Earth planet for millions of years. She creates death, destruction and world-shaking problems wherever she walks. She is the consort of Kal Niranjan, king of the negative worlds. Her name differs with the languages of the Earth and various

157

religions. For example, she is known to the Hindu religion as the Shakti, the female power who resides at the Kanth chakra, the consort of Kal Niranjan, whose other name is Brahm. Their sons are the famous Hindu trinity — Brahma, Vishnu and Shiva. Out of the union of these two parts of the negative current, the universal mind power, are the three subordinate currents which flow into the lower worlds and to these are attributed the creation of the lower worlds.

The Shat-Dal is the guardian of the music of the lower worlds. She oversees the music which is the actual lure of the astral influences on the psychic body of man. The second chakra which it affects besides the Indri at the base of the spine is the Nabhi chakra which is at a point near the solar plexus and influences this body of central nerves with upsets and charged emotions. This is the reason whenever anyone is upset in any manner or is disturbed he feels hungry and most of those who have had an affair of the heart are always hungry.

The negative hierarchy is of vast importance to the whole spiritual universe of God because it is the means which God has established for Soul to have Its education and testing in the lower worlds. It is the world of experience for Soul so It can become perfected in time.

However, the whole of the worlds are built upon the ECK, the audible life current. It is the highest and most sacred aspect of the SUGMAD, for it is the SUGMAD, and this alone accounts for the fact that we often call the heavenly music of God the WORD. All life is established on this music, or WORD of God. The ECK, therefore, is the Way, and is the path which every ECK Master has taught was the way back to God. Without this heavenly music, or the WORD, no one can reach God again. All the ECK Masters have taught this, and all the chelas who have reached any of the higher planes have traveled this path of the sacred sound current to God. They ride upon IT, and IT draws them up and carries them into the heavenly worlds for the supraspiritual experience.

The heavenly music, or what we call the ECK, is part of every sound of music which can be heard on any plane in the universe. When we hear it as martial music, or pop, it is only a degeneration of the heavenly music. It is using a different vehicle in this world, that of matter, in order to express itself. These types of music are only the outer bodies of the real sounds of God. Few, if any, ever realize that state in which they can possibly hear and understand the heavenly music. This unworldly state of music is so strange to the mortal mind of those who have heard, or can hear it with the spiritual ears, that they do not know exactly what it is. Sometimes it drives one out of his mind.

In other words, it is a dissent music. Frankly, all wars are created by the martial dissent music which is an offshoot of the heavenly music in the lower worlds. It strikes the astral body and stirs up the emotions of loyalty, violence and heroics.

Men hardly want freedom; it is too heavy a burden. Rather only about five percent of the human race seem to possess that additional enterprise and purpose that constitutes the evolutionary drive. It is this five percent that wants freedom.

The rest of mankind wants to be coddled, loved and taken care of like children. This is why certain types of music like the old ballads, the folk songs, and some aspects of rock and roll seem to be accepted, especially among the older people.

Rock and roll is compulsive as all primitive music is. The beat of the music is what disturbs the audience. It gets into the aura of the person and hangs there like the entities that are around the saloons and bars. It destroys the will of the individual and makes a slave of him.

Music can affect the pulse. We know that it was not until the late Roman Empire that certain observations began to be recorded, largely by Cassiodorus, a physician, who found that music affected the pulse. He used soft music to stop diarrhea and vomiting and advocated sweet and spiritual music as a prophylaxis against epidemics.

In general, slow minor tunes decrease the pulse. Jazz has been found to cause a more rapid rate than classical music. A lullaby decreases the pulse. Sad songs, as well as gay songs, can increase the pulse rate. The Marseillaise, a galop and the polka increase the pulse rate. Rock and roll acts like a narcotic on the individual. The only trouble here is that rock and roll becomes compulsive for the listener.

Rock and roll is part of the black arts. Purposely designed by the Kal forces, it is used to establish an illusion among the young and those interested that this is a better thing. The songs about freedom are, too, an illusion for one never has freedom in the human state of consciousness.

We know that each and every man when properly trained by the Living ECK Master is able to detach himself from the physical body while still living in that body and then can travel to all parts of the outlying universe.

Therefore he finds no freedom in this life. None in drugs, fanaticism, sociology, politics. What he sees as hypocrisy and the establishment only brings about dissatisfaction with the daily world. He turns to music like rock and roll to prove that he is part of the revolution to bring down the power structure, only to find that he has suddenly been deceived and trapped by something greater than himself and eventually ends as a definite part of that which he hates.

Good music is a living language. But generally unless one has the ability to Soul travel and listen to the heavenly music, it is composed by human beings. Thus human beings have to adapt themselves to shifting conditions and time and, like languages, it must constantly require new words and expressions so the next generation can understand.

Plato was somewhat of a prophet when he said that the introduction of a new style of music had to be shunned as it imperiled the nation. That is, styles of music are never disturbed without affecting the most important institutions of the state.

He explained that the new style of music quietly insinuates itself into the manners and customs and from these it issues a greater force which goes on to attack laws and constitutions, displaying the utmost imprudence, until it ends by overturning everything, both in public and in private.

The electronic music played by the youth groups is vulgar music. It is a sign of the times that vulgarity has taken over the artistic values and culture of the youth generation of our present age.

Western music has always had peculiar properties produced by social factors in the development of occidental societies. The basic factor of our society is the change in the social behavior, from the Protestant Ethics to the Freudian doctrine, from what is known in everyday idiom as the adjusted to the maladjusted personality — for example, from the rational to the vulgar. All this, of course, has a definite influence on music which is part of the social life of man. It is interwoven into his life patterns until he is an integral part of it and it has a deep effect upon his whole actions and deeds in his family, community and national life.

For some reason we believe that music and art of any nature are separated from the main stream of life, that each is an entity which is entirely of its own. While this is true, at the same time music and each of its fellow aspects of the cultural life of man are as much a part of the social life of a nation as politics, economics, religion, ethics, and law and order.

Prosperity, like that of the painters, has changed nothing in the musician's way of working. But the composer appears to have a more difficult lot of troubles on the financial end of the road. Today's crisis in musical style — for music has a style crisis just as painting has — may be better resolved by economic descriptions, sociological studies of the market, and reflections about political theories than by aesthetic reasoning.

The history of our musical language from early Christian psalmody through today's arithmetical abstractions is a long story. From the late eighteenth century, which witnessed music at its classical best, to the electronic guitar, we find the mystical idea which few can understand. It is less in the music today which is played for the popular ear. But then one has to remember that we are dealing with music which has been mainly for the arousing of the astral emotions. This includes the psalms which were put to music for church services or the sacred music by the famous Bach which are

161

today the classic hymns for most religious services. This also includes the hymns and verses sung by the orthodox religions of the East, i.e., Hinduism and Buddhism.

A very interesting point to be made is that in the jazz piece "The No-Name Jive" by Cab Calloway, a popular orchestra leader during the 1930s in this country, there is a high note hit here. During one part of the musical rendition the cornet section starts on a very low note and builds higher and higher until it reaches the peak of the musical note, then drops off and the bass instruments take over with a deep bottom note.

This is very interesting because it represents the chanting method used by the ECK chela with the word SUGMAD. He begins with the lower sound and starts building higher and higher ending on the highest pitch of sound possible with the letter "D", the last character in the ECK'S name of the Lord. Then he drops off and starts over again with the bottom or bass pitch and starts the building up again. The human system cannot stand the high pitches for it strains the vocal chords to chant it too long in this manner.

Another piece of music which comes under the category is that which is called the "Johnson Rag", another jazz rendition. It has a definite influence on the psychic body like other noises whether they have been put to some sort of rhythm or not.

However, it is well known that loud noises, such as rock and roll, are harmful to the heart, blood vessels, digestion and nervous system. Exposure to loud noises can harm the human body, say most medical authorities who have done research in this field. Preliminary studies indicate that weeks of exposure to high noise levels, such as encountered by workers in factories or on construction jobs, can elevate cholesterol levels and increase the build up of harmful fatty substances in the blood.

This is true of those who use the electric guitar today in the rock and roll music. Musicians of this nature will soon find that constant loud and often inharmonious music will bring about certain ailments. The effect on the blood vessels is thought to be particularly dangerous in individuals whose

162

arteries are already narrowed by arteriosclerosis, which is a condition where deposits of fatty substances are in the arteries.

There is also the known effect of short term exposure to noise which has the same effect on the body as does stress and anxiety. According to some medical authorities it is revealed that the heart beats faster, blood vessels constrict, pupils dilate, the head turns, the skin pales, and the stomach, esophagus and intestines are seized by spasms. When the noises or music are prolonged, there are heart flutters that eventually subside when the noise diminishes.

This is why many musicians have to turn to drugs, pot and other means of escape in order to survive their career in the music world. This is especially true in the non-classical field of music.

Contemporary music is all things to all people, but to the young generation it is used as a total escape from reality. The reason for the tremendous loudness of modern popular music is to destroy communication. The music of youth has always been to express the inability of young people to face life. For them music has become not a way of life, but a way of escaping from life. However, music which is melodious and with harmony contributes to the health of the body and mind. Music and the sounds of instruments quicken the circulation of the blood which passes off the waste matter more readily.

There are some cases, even in the Middle Ages, where persons being seized by violent illnesses were given the use of musicians and their music instead of the consultations of physicians. The musicians soon brought such individuals back on their feet with the harmony of their instruments.

Plato, as mentioned before, wrote that disturbing the styles of music affects the most important institutions in a whole nation as the new style insinuates itself into the manners and customs changing both the public and private lives of the nation. It becomes a greater force which attacks laws and constitutions, modes of dress, moral codes and habits. The truth of this can readily be seen in the world today as the changing styles of music seem to affect the very way of life from one generation to another.

Plato might have been writing about the rock and roll riots of the fifties and sixties, and if he were living in our age would argue that jazz and swing music are responsible for most of the world's troubles.

We find then that the musician is an instrument for the higher powers, whether it be the ECK or the Kal. We can play or compose music from out of the psychic worlds, or allow that which is the spiritual flow to use us for the uplifting of mankind. Thus we see that Cesar Auguste Franck was the composer and musician whose works bridged the spiritual and the material worlds. On the other hand, the Richard Wagner music has been one which has served to bring about revolutionary changes in the world societies. Also we can consider Stravinsky whose music has had a deep influence on the mental and emotional bodies of man and brought sharp changes to the stable social orders of the western world.

The musician usually functions in the field of emotions rather than in the mind, although Bach appeals to the mental body of man more than any of the classical musicians. This within itself, whether the musician is creative or interpretative, frequently uses him to find himself at the mercy of those very emotions which he is endeavoring to sway in others. Being recognized exponents of the emotions, and constantly meeting others who view them in that light, their personality becomes subject to emotional vortices which few musicians are capable of understanding or controlling since they lack the power consciously to resist the turbulent thought forms directed at them.

Such powers of resistance can be only acquired by an ECKist who has at least reached the fifth (true Soul) plane, for then a measure of control over his own lower vehicles has been attained and this in itself is not easy, for the average successful musician is endowed with the positive virtues of his inner bodies, as opposed to the negative ones of the average man, hence those disturbances which often assail his emotional nature which is located in his astral body.

The exacting sounds of the audible life current which we know as the ECK, or any of its aspects, is a new science in the western world. Few if any composers and musicians can discriminate between the innumerable influences which music and sound can open in the subtle bodies of an audience, both individually and collectively. Therefore, a composer finds himself on an uncharted sea while awaiting the singular inspiration which will strike up an harmonious chord.

The classical musician receives through himself as an open channel that which transmits to his audience an uplifting force and inspires to greater actions in this life. On the other hand, those musicians who deal only with the psychic forces may do everything in reverse. Their music appeals to the base nature of man and brings him into the lower emotions which could cause harm and damage. However, in both cases the musician's responsibility is great, and yet for the most part he is unaware of what he is doing and the influence on his listeners.

Popular music has been since the beginning of time that which has been simply commercial. It is written, composed and played for the younger audiences whose emotional bodies have not been developed. It is composed and played for the dollar, and this is exhibited in the amount of sales of records throughout the countries of the world.

This is a far cry from those days when music was associated with religions and the priests played an important part in its development and systematizing society. The early ECK masters were able to hear the music of the ECK and to them came the answer that harmony was the answer of the SUGMAD to man's plea for peace and happiness.

The ECK masters have discovered the influence of music upon the subtle bodies of man brought about by mantras, and realized that if certain notes were constantly repeated as in the Zikar, spiritual results would be attained and definite powers would be brought into action in both the inner and outer worlds.

During the early civilizations, including those of Lemuria,

165

commonly known as Mu, the Atlantis and the Inca empires, including those which were far in the past beyond these, the influence of the ECK initiates used sound to build the beautiful and wonder-inspiring forms. But in the later phases of these mighty empires, as the black magicians took over, the Sound or Word, as it is often known, came to be used as a force of destruction. Discordant sounds were deliverately used to shatter and disintegrate. The discordant sounds were practiced to gain power over the people and the result brought the downfall of these magnificent empires.

It is well-known among the ECK masters that Claude Debussy, the French composer, was among the first of the composers to introduce the overtones of the ancient empires, especially Atlantis. He was unconsciously used by the ECK masters to bring back again nature music, thus turning entirely away from the human element to perform this mission. He began at the first rung of the elemental evolutionary ladder and brought forth the music of the gnomes, the fairies, the water spirits, and the spirits of the clouds and fire.

Maurice Ravel followed Debussy's idea and did a variation of the latter's music. Ravel, in fact, did somewhat of an extension bridging the gap between the nature-spirits and the first rung of the entities and beings who inhabit the emotional area of the astral world. After the advent of the music of both musicians there was a broad change in the attitude toward the invisible worlds and spiritual matters in the press and popular publications.

If the Living ECK Master thinks it is fit to do so, he encourages and lifts the consciousness of those who are musically talented, as well as others who are capable of other talents into the knowledge of how to become a vehicle for the ECK. But there is always the safeguard on these talented ones, for should the knowledge they gain become general and give some the feeling that this can be used for the acquisition of personal power, they would repeat the mistakes and errors of those musicians of the early continents which brought about a drowning by the seas.

166

Those who have talent and try to use the MAHANTA, the Living ECK Master, or the ECK either in ignorance or knowingly, suffer in the end with terrible disasters. It is during the present era that we find so much of this being done, as many go to India to find a teacher who will give them a mantra which is believed to bring greater material results. Sacred music put to swing and the Sounds of the ECK brought into music that results finally in discordance brings about misery to the human race.

The mantra are handed down through the centuries by the ECK masters to individual chelas who have followed them. Some of these have become entirely associated with religious traditions, and performed at set times of the day. There would be a chant to be sung before the early morning contemplation, another for noon, and still another for the evening contemplation. Each have been calculated to have a specific effect upon the singer and audience alike.

The ECK masters in those early times did not seek to merely develop music as an art, but sought to enhance its mantramistic value to those chelas who had taken up the study of ECKANKAR. Contemplative by nature, and having realized that certain sequences of musical notes produce profound effects, they were experimented with until they received the desired results; that result was the ECKSHAR, or the superconscious trance state. Within this state the chela should be able to hear the music of the ECK, which is sometimes called the "music of vision". This is said to be the bliss state and is blissful enough for those who have reached it to believe they have reached the ultimate state of all states.

This music affected mainly that known as the Atma (Soul) body but it did not bring out the tonal uplift for the masses because it wasn't revealed in this manner. To reach the masses it had to become music which was somewhat understood, through both the mind and emotions. This meant that the mantra touched only those who were interested and could lift them into the higher states. But it had no appeal for the average man because of a lack of certain elements such as physical vitalities and power. Often,

167

unless used properly, it made the chela one sided, inert and unequally balanced in character as it has so many in the Indian race of that Asian subcontinent.

Whether the chela who follows a psychic teacher or a so-called master knows it or not, he must be careful in chanting the mantra or else he becomes that person who lacks energy, lacks power and finds himself gradually growing toward neurosis. In other words, mantra are somewhat dangerous unless the chela is under a skilled and well trained spiritual master, like the MAHANTA, the Living ECK Master.

An examination of ancient religion reveals the fact that schools for the study of esotericism existed, and still exist, in almost every civilization. These schools were called the mystery cults and one of their most important ceremonies was the initiation where the candidate with the aid of music and other rites was put into a trance from which he emerged with knowledge of those states beyond this world.

We find here something very strange going on, that is, that the Indians (Hindu) have used four divisions to the musical note, the modern western music has only two, while at the same time the third tone of the early Egyptian mystery schools seems to have been able to produce a greater result in loosening the emotional body from the physical and producing an astral trance. At the same time we find that the Greeks in their mystery schools used the half-tone which worked on the physical plane.

This means the Indians developed their mental bodies through the type of music which they played. The Egyptians had their music for the development of the psychic (astral) body and the Greeks used their music for the development of the physical. In this survey we can have the fact that the Romans, although they had little use for music except for entertainment of their deities and music for their armies, used it for the development of the base natures, that is, pertaining to war and conquest.

The development of the vortices in the human aura is that in which we should be interested. It is the lack of what music there is which causes the vortices to become fixed in one way

168

with the individual and national aura. These vortices are small whirling holes in the aura, similar to a whirlwind or a whirlpool, but the effects of sound upon them will develop them into larger effects, or smaller, depending on the type of music. They should not be there at all, and the more there are and the larger they are, will cause a lack in the individual traits, such as bringing about a set pattern in the society, or individual, lethargy, lack of concrete knowledge, or misused power.

It was through Greece that we came to the half-tone and into European music. It, of course, worked especially on the material and physical levels. It can be seen here that as the music of the ECK became audible to man it passed from the subtle to the less subtle and finally to the gross. Below this, music can no longer be called music, but merely sound or noise.

The Greeks adopted several of the instruments from the East and from the Egyptians, but following this such leaders as Plato and Pythagoras found that music was the foundation to a nation's strength and the positiveness of the individual. The base music of the Middle Eastern countries, like Babylon, the Medes, and Persia, created such baseness in the national character of their empires that it was responsible for the orgies for which they became famous.

However, the Greeks bypassed most of this and laid the groundwork for western music. Not until the Middle Ages did music begin to find itself in the higher octaves again. But here we see that such chant, as the Gregorian chant which developed, created such a power in the church that it was centuries before the action of other music could make any headway against resolving the Christian church.

The third tone of the Egyptian music was a strong factor in bringing about a perversion of their occult sciences which were built on power that fell when the third tone became too influential in breaking up the stable power of the Pharoahs. The same happened with Greece, in their love of beauty, as the half-tone of their nation's music brought about a cult based on physical beauty which declined under the same methods as the Egyptians. Rome fell through a similar perversion which turned out to be a cult of manliness, and its music brought about disastrous results.

Music and the lack of it contributed to the dark ages of Europe. The discordant music and the troubadours, which the Crusaders brought back with them from the Middle Eastern countries, helped to pave the way for modern music during the reformation period.

Three composers, Orlandus Lassus, Palestrina, and Monteverde, who lived during the sixteenth century, brought about deep changes in the stability of the western nations with their music. They in a sense became instruments for the ECK power which began to raise man into his higher consciousness again.

It is found that their music not only led to the split in the church, but later came about in a subtle way to create a deeper conflict between the church and the people during the seventeenth century in France, and planted the first stake of the conflict which ultimately became the winds of terror known as the French revolution.

The organ was developed in England under Henry VII, and brought about the split between his son Henry VIII and the church to form the Church of England. This was followed by the anti-Puritan music that created the Civil War between the Loyalists and the Puritans and brought Cromwell into power.

The line of music both destructive and positive has been somewhat outlined here into the modern age. The future says that the influence of music will bring about benefits to those who can accept them, but eventually the discordant elements will cause the end of the material worlds in its last cycle, the Kali Yuga, to prepare man again for the Golden Age to come and the next MAHANTA, the Living ECK Master, who will serve mankind throughout the next cycle of time.

THE PRICE OF
THE SPIRITUAL LIFE

The attitude of the religionist today is that he must build popular concepts of God and His divine promises into his audience or suffer from a lack of followers.

Among these promises appears to be the deliberate misrepresentation that the life of the spiritual acolyte is an easy one, provided he has made contact with the God force, that once this is done his general welfare, both physical and spiritual, will be greatly enhanced.

The greatest promise is that the acolyte can have anything in his life because with God nothing is impossible. The miracle can be performed and all of us can be changed from the ugly duckling into a Cinderella or Prince Charming, from poverty to a position of wealth.

However, we are told that the condition of having all these promises fulfilled is to have God in our life. That once this happens there will be free gifts showered upon us like rain from heaven, and in no way will we have to pay for what we get.

This is an affront to the dignity of anyone who seeks God in his life for the sake of having God. It is an act of dishonesty to preach that we can have anything from God without some form of payment. It simply is not true for as long as we are in this physical universe, wearing a human body, we must make payment for all things, whether they be spiritual or material.

No person can honestly promise that the path to God is going to be easy. It is certain that no ECK master is going to involve himself in such an outrageous untruth with his own followers by promising them that should they follow the path of ECK that God is going to distribute His gifts freely to all on an equal basis.

171

We can only receive the gifts of the Supreme Being in accordance with our own state of spiritual development, and there is always a price attached to whatever is received from God. Many think too seriously in the matter of material payment, although this is one way of handling compensation.

It is a general belief among many who follow the path of religions that we can merely receive the gift and not give in return. This is an illusion established by the Kal (negative) forces. It has created more problems among the acolytes than any other particular one which could arise while traveling the illuminated way to the heart of God.

Among the modern religious teachings are the preconceived notions that God takes care of the good and sends His wrath upon the wicked. That anyone who obeys the moral laws will receive all His grace and abundant health and prosperity. The whole key to this sort of teaching lies in a failure of consciousness of those who are striving for the material end alone, for God cares little for the physical and material embodiments which exist in this world. He is interested in the preservation of the individuality of Soul.

If so many things seem to be unjust in this physical world it is for the reason that it is ruled by the Kal (negative) powers. But this is all for a purpose for God created all the lower worlds to be the training grounds and the educational academy for the spiritualization of each Soul sent here. The buffets and hardships that we encounter in this world are to train and perfect Soul so it will eventually become ready for a specific mission. This is to become a co-worker with God.

Therefore we must pass through incarnation after incarnation experiencing every type of trial and tribulation known in the lower worlds. When we have passed through the ordeal of fire and water one becomes a perfect channel for the ECK. He has learned the hard way and knows that for every gift that the divine SUGMAD has bestowed upon him has been paid for in sweat, blood, tears and ecstasy.

When we study the lives of the great spiritual giants who have walked the Earth it is shown how they suffered deeply in order to gain the spiritual gifts of God. All were grateful

172

for the smallest grace received, and humbly beseeched Him for the supernatural state of life. Many lived in rags, half-starved at times and sometimes begging for food and mauled by the public. The world has treated so many of them with scorn, exterminating most of them by different methods of cruelty. But never once do we read of any complaint arising from the lips of these magnificent men of God.

They accepted the trials of life as the spiritual experiences to perfect Soul and lift them into the higher realms of God. When Socrates, that great Greek, whose name is a household word in every nation of the world, would return home in the evenings after spending the day teaching the youth of Athens of a better life, his wife would berate him and sometimes beat him. He was patient and took the punishment with grace for being so much greater than her in spiritual unfoldment, and knew that this was the ordeal of fire that he was experiencing in this world. He knew upon taking the cup of hemlock poison that the gift of God must be paid for in some manner even though it meant his death. He drank it cheerfully while praising his gods.

It is the karma of the human state of consciousness that we pay for everything within this world, be it spiritual or materialistic. All the outer works of the master must be accepted for a price, be it in service, remuneration or donation.

Some cults and metaphysical movements outwardly declare a policy against payment, but this is not a natural means of reaching the true spiritual depths of the individual. One finds here the lack of consideration for the law of life which has two elements within it necessary to the human state. These are health and currency. If we have neither our physical life suffers, and if we have one and not the other we are out of balance. No one should put his time and attention on either of these, but they are necessary for the upkeep of the human body. If the body does not receive care then it suffers and we are in a state of dis-ease.

The main point here is that we should not become

attached to either of these two elements of the human life. We must be able to detach ourselves from the emotional part of the materialistic necessities, either to take them or leave them.

We have two sides of the spiritual works, often called the outer and the inner. We can say that they are the physical and esoteric teachings, and while one pays in coin in the physical for the outer works, the inner is taught by revelation and no price tag can be exacted for the divine knowledge that comes to him who listens and understands.

Anyone who steps out on the path of ECK must remember that life will exact from him a retribution for whatever he puts into it. If he gives nothing, then he will receive nothing from life. But if he gives to life, then all life will give abundantly in return.

We receive according to what we pay for in the realm of God.

THE KANDJUR
The Words and Wisdom of Paul Twitchell

INTRODUCTION

When a small boy discovers that he can leave his physical body at will, the experience might prove so terrifying as to turn him into an incurable neurotic. Such was not the case with Paul Twitchell, who made this discovery very early in his career. He went on to lead a normal life, to serve as an officer in the U.S. Navy, and to devote all his spare time for many years to the study of phenomena beyond the bounds of ordinary sensory perception.

His researches led him to learn speed-reading, by which he was enabled to digest an incredible number of books on an unbelievable number of subjects. It was after delving deeply into history, philosophy, ethics and religion that he was able to determine the underlying basis for the spiritual power he had long recognized in himself and as being latent in others.

India, he found, possessed the greatest store of such knowledge. Thither he went for study under a noted master, Sudar Singh. And it was in India that there occurred the second revelation which was to result in his becoming a world-renowned teacher and savant.

He met a singular individual: Rebazar Tarzs. This person stood apart from other gurus as a mountain towers over an anthill. There was about him a perfect aura of spiritual knowledge and power.

Paul Twitchell became his chela, and over the years Rebazar Tarzs poured forth to his student the secret wisdom and techniques by which supposedly earth-bound mortals could enter consciously into the stream of eternal truth which has flowed through the physical and spiritual universe ever since (or even since before) creation.

Paul Twitchell found the way hard, the studies exacting, but he emerged the most highly finished master of this ancient and secret knowledge whom the world is to know during this age.

175

Rebazar Tarzs told him that his mission in his present life was to serve as the Living ECK Master for the modern world, to bring to a confused and materialistic era an ages-old message, the message of ECK.

ECK, that slender yet unbreakable thread of truth running throughout eternity, tells us that each individual is a spiritual entity who will never die, and who need not lose his individuality nor be forced to return to earthly existence through interminable reincarnations in order to work off his karma.

While intimately aware of these precious secrets through his study, the teachings of Rebazar Tarzs and his own experiences, Paul Twitchell yet delayed in bringing them to the world out of an innate reluctance to appear to be setting himself above other men — for all men, he knew, contained intrinsically the same powers as he did. It required a series of visits by his old mentor (in his Soul body) to force open the flood of insight which has recently flowed from Paul Twitchell's mouth and pen.

In the few short years since he began the public exposition of ECKANKAR — the pathway to ECK — this amazing man has set thousands on the road to full recognition of their own natures as spiritual beings. The influence of his teachings has reached hundreds of thousands — probably millions — of confused mortals, and has lifted them up and given them a whole new attitude toward life.

It may well be that Paul Twitchell and ECKANKAR have come to redeem the world of men in this moment of dire despair from the deadly materialism by which its very existence is threatened from moment to moment. Many believe so; let us all fervently hope so.

In the following pages are quotations from Paul Twitchell's talks and writings on his sacred and all-important subject. If approached with care, respect and concentration, their effect upon the reader is certain to be remarkable.

ECKANKAR, the ancient science of Soul travel, is the key to the heavenly worlds. The spiritual freedom which is gained by reaching these rarefied states, in which we dwell when God-Realization is attained, is not describable by words.

Only when man loosens and lets himself surrender to the Supreme Deity does he find himself guided to liberation, or salvation of Soul. Out of this comes total freedom, total awareness and total responsibility.

The Zurich, Switzerland Lectures
July, 1967

The no-freedom state takes a heavy toll on brain power and leaves the individual without any motivation to seek God. Thus the individual suffers, the family suffers, and the community and state reap the dubious reward of negating their citizens. Neither has any society in world history made any progress when its own people were forced to live in it without freedom.

The Berlin Lectures
July, 1967

The ECK society is the only one within the social structures of the world nations which is not aberrated. We are living in a heteroclitic social structure and must recognize this throughout the globe. Only the ECK chelas are living in a spiritually sane world of their own, developing their own society and culture.

The California Parapsychology Foundation
Lectures, San Diego, Calif., March, 1965

Perfection has no limitation nor is it temporary or changeable, while pleasure and suffering are the conditions of material existence.

The Ancient Creed of ECKANKAR
Orion Magazine, Nov.-Dec., 1965

Truth is for those who take the time and trouble to seek it out. The ECK Master knows of the hidden side of God which has existed as a knowledge distinct from the science and philosophy of those who have written the sacred scriptures or caused their disciples to record their masters's words.

177

Why are those who know or possess this knowledge unwilling to let it pass into general circulation for the sake of a better and more successful struggle against deceit, evil and ignorance? Knowledge is never concealed from the eyes of the masses. The fact is that the enormous majority of people do not want knowledge; they refuse their share of it and do not even take the rations allotted to them.

The Flute of God

The human factor is always the cause of trouble in the physical world. It crops up steadily like Hamlet's conscience, and like this character in Shakespeare's tragedy we wrestle with the conscience until it destroys us. But this destruction comes only in the mental world, and if man would place his attention on the spiritual he would never have to be bothered with the lower states of scruples and morals. For then the ECK would take care of all things and guide him rightly through all obstacles of life into the heart of God.

Long Beach, California Lectures
November, 1967

All spiritual works require creativeness, for creativity is the basis of love. Love itself is hardly anything more than this.

The Southwest Seminar
Dallas, Texas, 1967

I will leave you. Nevertheless all who have become the followers of ECK during my stay here will find the divine teachings are carried on from the planes beyond this material world. Hence, as the ECK I am with you always, no matter on what level of life you may be.

Dialogue in Rome, Italy
July, 1968

Revelation is the basis of the divine life in God. Until we recognize this the life of man is in chaos. He keeps seeking outside himself, never learning that as a channel of God it is within his grasp to have the light and sound here and now.

The Helsinki Talks
June, 1968

ECK is always in conflict with religion and philosophy. It is never reconciled with anything in the physical and mental universe. It is only when the chela takes himself into the spiritual world that he recognizes that Soul awareness is part of the truth of God, and that this is the domain of ECK.

Conversation in Darjeeling, India
May, 1957

The ECK must come first in the life of every initiate, regardless of what he believes otherwise. If it does not, then he is wasting his time in the spiritual works. IT will demand more and more of you until IT will have every part of your being, including your heart, mind and Soul.

Dialogue in Mexico City
February, 1963

The personal factor in the ECK force is that IT works in everyone's life in the very minute detail of their daily affairs. We only have to stand aside and let IT go to work and produce the miracles which IT can do for all.

Private Dialogue in Jamaica
May, 1965

It is certainly true, certainly noticeable, that after one becomes an initiate, he is no longer interested in being free to live a bland and comfortable routine. He knows that life never works out this way for an ECK initiate. He soon learns that more hardships, adventure and spiritual understanding come from life in the higher worlds. He has a greater desire than ever for the spiritual nectar of God.

London Lectures
June, 1967

I am often asked, how does one as an individual guard against all the various difficulties which are bound to come up, not only in the outer personality, but on all levels — emotional, mental, spiritual. The answer lies in this: does one's everyday life reflect what can be called functional happiness? That is to say, is one really happy with what one is doing and does this show itself in one's intimate relationships and daily life? This is the yardstick for

179

measuring whether one is on the right track or not, and it doesn't matter what others say about us, however wonderful, if the daily life of the individual does not demonstrate the good life: for if we are overtired, frustrated, haven't the time for things, there is an imbalance and this is wrong.

Talks with Friends
Florence, Italy, 1968

The basic principle in ECK is that which states that at one time or another all bodies within this physical atmosphere must come to rest.

Therefore, Soul Travel is based upon this whole principle. If Soul inhabits a body here in this world, it must learn to leave it daily and dwell in the upper worlds, which is its true home. Some day the body will come to rest, or die, as is known to all who live here. Therefore, Soul should not let itself be trapped in this physical environment. The only way out is through ECK.

The Spiritual Notebook

ECK has its responsibility to give liberation of Soul to every nation, and to every individual in this tired old world. IT is the only legitimate spiritual force today. IT is the divine legal power, authorized only by the Supreme Deity.

Dialogue in Honolulu
February, 1961

The reason that no one can defeat the ECK is that when we think of IT, we think of something already here. IT is created by spiritual tradition, by spiritual history, and by the SUGMAD. IT is perfect but IT is not simplified.

Talks in Miami Beach
December, 1968

No path to God is of any consequence without revelation through Soul travel. Too many believe they can reach the heavenly worlds via the passive state. This is the illusion that the Kal power establishes in order to pacify the seeker. All who reach this state know this and do it by being bold and adventurous.

First World Wide Seminar
October, 1967

180

Education is only learning to frame one's will in accordance with events. We should not strive to change what happens, but to change ourselves, to be free under any conditions. The art of life for every person is his own life in the ECK.

Private Talks in Athens
July, 1968

God does not seek worshippers except in spirit and in truth. Therefore, we must look to the subtle part of ourselves to find this spirit and truth which are the mediums through which to adore and worship the Almighty One. None can do this in the flesh, for when the body is gone, what does God care about a corpse and a few quarts of blood? He is more concerned with our survival as Soul. He sees to it that we survive through all eternity via the Soul body.

The Medford, Oregon Lectures
April, 1968

The life of ECK depends on its collective spiritual consciousness and not on movement, not upon anything in this world of economy and physical matter. After we learn that ECK is the life force of all things, then we start learning that IT has no form or size or rules. IT turns out to be what we least expect. So we can expect anything while traveling the spiritual path of ECK. We don't put our private rules and evaluations on people, places or events. None can put his own order in the universe, except through mathematics. Where we are heading for in the upper spiritual realms, everything is upside down and sideways.

The Tucson, Arizona Lectures
August, 1967

St. Peter was an ordinary fisherman, and St. Francis was a rich man's son. In time of stress, anyone from any level may rise if he is needed by the Supreme Deity.

You are curious to know who I am. This I will not tell you, but from my deeds you shall know me, for it is the fruit and not the vine by which all shall know me. I am only a humble instrument for God and want you to recognize this much about me.

Dialogue in Capetown
October, 1956

ECK is my only staff to help me through life, through what remains to me of the pilgrimage of existence. Without IT we fall into the world of Kal, the illusionary veil, which keeps us in darkness and ignorance. We cannot yield to the worldly powerful but must accept the staff of life, which is ECK, to guide us. It is bread for the hungry, water for the thirsty, and the staff for the weary and burdened.

Copenhagen Lectures
June, 1967

Those who know the ECK masters have called them "Sons of God," but more often the "Manifestation of God" in the physical flesh. Each must come through the maya (the veil of flesh) as Jesus did when born of Mary. It is God's own way of working through worldly instruments to give the true message to all, to give each a splinter of truth. There is nothing to give, nothing to receive, only to know.

Dialogues in Sidney, Australia
February, 1951

The need for spiritual work is universally human. Any individual who assumes he can live without spiritual advancement is caught in a self-deceptive trap. Only through the ECK traveler of the worlds beyond can one find success in the works of the SUGMAD.

The Supreme Message can be revealed ultimately to those in the simple heart. Its starting point lies where truth pushes aside the cloak of illusion and becomes the shining inspiration to the Initiates of ECK. The link-up with the essence of the SUGMAD, the spiritual word, gives the Initiate an insight into the great mysteries of Heaven and Earth.

The Spiritual Notebook

The weakness of the human consciousness is that we do not realize that we make our own laws or considerations, but generally we follow out what somebody else, or a society, has given us. The root of all success, be it spiritual or material, is this: we make our own laws and follow them out, and if anything goes wrong, then we are to blame ourselves and nobody else.

Letter to A Chela
Philadelphia, Pa., May, 1962

It has been stated that ECK is the All-Embracing Force of life of which our whole elemental living is made up within the worlds of God. Those seeking the Ultimate Experience, that which we call God-Realization, have no judgment of what path to take. This statement is made because most individuals do not have a criterion by which to judge their inner experiences. We live too much in the external, the outer and objective viewpoint, to know much about the inner life and its effects upon our spiritual behavior.

The Spiritual Notebook

When comes a man who breaks away from all human interests and spiritual interests of the world's races, he is often hailed as a saviour of mankind. More than likely he will be denounced by the orthodox leaders of his day. He will not have many followers, and those who do follow will likely be zealots. Yet to hold them together for a spiritual interest like ECK, he must lower his standards and do miracles. Thus he will be called the Wayshower, for he has established an archetype of the Reality and the only true path to God.

The Edinburgh Talks
June, 1967

He who follows the wisdom of ECK dwells in the Heart of God, and is beyond all goodness and evil. None shall touch him, for he is free of all worldly things.

Shariyat-Ki-Sugmad

Since the ECK Master must work with all those who are willing to be with him in studying the science of Soul Travel, in helping them to connect with the ECK power that flows from him into themselves, he must show them they can seek no further. This means the ECK touches the chela quickly as he makes contact with the Master for the first time, and will start working out his karma and problems on various planes. In other words, the ECK will begin to lift that Soul into the higher planes. Many times he will not recognize this fact, but he certainly knows that something is taking place for his own benefit. His mind is clearing and the material aspects of his life are making gains instead of losses. His spiritual life seems to be progressing, whereas it was at a standstill.

First World Wide Seminar
Las Vegas, October, 1967

There is no reason to believe that the forces of ECK should ever engage themselves in the social structure of the world. The orthodox church can make changes under pressure, but cannot do everything; evan a religion like the Catholic faith with its vast membership, or Buddhism which claims powers over the lives of its faithful, spends too much time saying NO to its followers. Such faiths are not, of course, neutral observers but are made up of men whose goal in life is creating social conditions and interfering in world affairs. ECK has no such interest, but only to reach the individual to get him out of this world.

Dialogue in Bangkok
April, 1951

Some feel that all men share an interest in a single goal, because it is the Will of God and is suggested to us by our reason. They feel that serving a common god is a service to God. This often gives people an interest in living. But those in ECK know this is not true. We know that God is only interested in survival of Soul, and not in the embodiment in the physical life, which has all the complexities of social problems and bodily troubles.

Dialogue in Lisbon
September, 1947

The true universal message cannot be given in its pure state via the physical channel, except by the ECK Master. By working through the Atma Sarup with the spiritual bodies of his chelas, he is able to bring the pure message of God to the world. This is essential to all who are walking the ECK path. We cannot use only outer form and have outer rituals to reach the higher stages of spiritual development. Nor can we have only the inner and expect to gain all esoteric knowledge and progress. We need both for fulfillment in establishing Soul in the heart of God.

First World Wide Seminar
Las Vegas, Nev., October, 1967

I have no reason to believe that a great amount of people will ever take much interest in ECK except when the social structure of a country is under attack, or the world is falling to pieces. It is doubtful whether they should. The existing minor hubbub of metaphysics, spiritualism, orthodox religions, philosophies, churches, sects and cults would become extinct if the Voice of ECK was raised to still the confusion which now exists.

The Spiritual Notebook

Everywhere I go the seeds of ECK are planted. First comes the upheaval of the social structure and political establishments; nations change, people become restive and agitation is everywhere. Then follows the destruction of all that is old, the negativity and the sickness of humanity. In its place is rebuilt the new, the spiritual growth of mankind and the beauty of life.

Talks in Calcutta, India
September, 1940

We are like the bovine creatures that think the grass is greener in the next field, and force our way through the fences to find that it is not as good. We run from one cult to another, study all forms of religions, look for truth in the far corners of the world, and wander aimlessly trying to find God. There is no place to go, there is no seeking of the Supreme Deity anywhere but right here. IT has never moved apart from us, but awaits our recognition of ITS presence; for we are always on solid ground regardless of where we are or what we are doing. The worst of sinners is as much in the presence of God as the great illuminated saint. The difference is recognition.

San Francisco Lectures
February, 1967

There will always be those who make claim to being Soul Travelers, those who will say they are the ECK Master and speak with the authority of God. Beware of them, for they are like the cunning animals of the field who live by stealth and knavery, who must steal the body and its senses away from God only to promote their own egotism and make others believe they are the true teachers of the spiritual works. They are creatures of the matter world and lower

185

astral plane. If you follow them, you also will become such creatures.

Talks in Manila, P.I.
October, 1948

The ECK Master does not need the world but the world needs him. He is the perfect instrument for the divine power which flows out of the Godhead into the worlds below. He always appears in the physical male body for the reason that within the spiritual consciousness the embodiment of any savant must be the male. Not the masculine form that we know from the human state, but that which is the spiritual state. Within this form of embodiment all the principles of God are merged in order to make the perfect Master, the Sat Guru, whose strength in the temple of flesh can administer the ECK power properly.

Dialogue in Venice, Italy
July, 1968

My greatest problem with people is dealing, not with skeptics or non-believers, but with those with failure-consciousness. A large number of people are imbued with feelings of inadequacy. This leads to cruelty, unhappiness, vanity, greed and many other ills of life. Little wonder, then, at the idea that all we need in this life to make things right is wealth and opulence which take care of the body and senses. So many persons have become rich and famous and have ridden the waves of popularity only to find that something was still escaping them, for the feeling of inadequacy was still there. This was the lack of God, the lack of true sincerity in life, which comes from leaning upon the Supreme Deity and nothing else. Until one learns to do this, the feeling of inadequacy will prevail.

Talks in Dublin, Ireland
August, 1928

The teachings of truth never come from the outside, but have to grow from within under the guidance and with the help of the ECK Master. Truth never pretends it has a monopoly on God. There are many ways to God and every Soul must be free to choose which one it prefers.

The Tiger's Fang

ECK is a wave, not a static thing as so many want to believe. For this reason we cannot put self-interest first. Our interest must be stronger for ECK than for anything else. This is especially true of the initiates who have a love for all which is more than that for a thousand parents put together. If your life is full of adversities, misfortunes and difficulties, it is due to the reactions of past karmas. But they are only passing phases. They come and go. The ECK is always, forever, with you, and it gives all spiritual help and protection.

Dialogue in Cairo, Egypt
May, 1956

Doubts and hesitations are two negative factors that always beset every true seeker after God. One seeks and finds and wonders if this is the true ECK Master. After a while he discovers that he has not contacted the perfect Master, but an imperfect one. His life goal becomes frustrated and he earnestly prays for the Sat Guru to come into his life. You may see the ECK Master in the flesh and recognize him, and then again, you may see him in your periods of silent devotions to God. But you will recognize him when you meet him.

The Glasgow, Scotland Talks
June, 1960

The ECK works for the benefit of all humanity, in all ages, but works through a human form as an electrical current uses the light bulb to give its light to all concerned. This means then that the ECK has always been the God-power that sustains the world. It uses savants, adepts and saints as the selected human poles. The greatest of all these is the chosen physical pole of the Living ECK Master who comes to guide Souls and show them the way back to God. The physical body passes away but the ECK never leaves.

Talks in Lisbon
June, 1958

The main point that I have to bring out to you is that the Kal (the negative) power will always try to defeat anyone in this physical state of life; this is its purpose. God established it for the very purpose of giving us spiritual experience in order to get back into heaven eventually as a spiritually matured Soul. And the more we make the effort for spiritual unfoldment, the more we try to travel the spiritual path, the greater the attack of Kal. It uses the human consciousness of those around us as its channel to make these attacks. So never be unhappy when things do not seem to put themselves together, but know this one thing: I am with you always, assisting you spiritually at all times, regardless of distance and time. This is possible for me to do with every chela under my care.

Private Talks in Lima, Peru
December, 1957

The ECK is that which unites all men under the banner of truth through ITSELF, but we will rise higher and go into the sublime for our personal contact with the divine light and voice of God. Soon we will be able to do this at will. To talk about truth is one thing, but to see and become conscious of it is above all experiences.

Los Angeles Lectures
February, 1968

Man should seek Self-Realization, God-Realization and Universality. This would give him an understanding of the SUGMAD, the Absolute Supreme Deity. IT is expressed in both Light and Sound. God is the Light and Sound principle. This is the true path to God which can be traveled only when one has taken up the works of ECK — when one has transcended the body consciousness. We have no words, no ideas which can describe it. It is worthless to speak or talk about it.

Personal Letter to a Chela
The Hague, Holland, June, 1967

Some persons get very impatient because they do not learn Soul Travel within the matter of a few discourses, and want to give up. In fact, I have letters from chelas who say, "I have had the first two discourses and practiced the exercises laid down in the Illuminated Way series, and am not able to do anything yet." I was some time with the ECK Master Sudar

Singh before he even began to show me the advanced work in ECK. I was tearing down everything which was believed to be right, and starting all over again. It took me years to learn so many things before I was selected to carry on the work of ECK.

Talks in Florence, Italy
July, 1968

There is but one power — the ECK power — which is the function of God reaching all His kingdoms and planes. This power works with and through a selected human pole and has two functions — the positive and negative. This is like electricity which can freeze water and burn fire simultaneously in different places. We find the incarnations of both powers, the positive and negative. The mission of the incarnates of the positive power is to assist the Soul to return to God by helping him to break the chains of the bonds of mind and matter. The mission of the negative power is to sustain and keep the world in order. It punishes the wicked, lifts the righteous of the religious orders and keeps the world in order. Those of the positive incarnates work for the reunion of Soul with God, and take him into the heart of God to become a co-worker.

Talks in Algiers
March, 1941

The works of ECK are based upon humility and love. These qualities are necessary for spiritual unfoldment on the ECK path to God. Love is the positive quality of man. It is the negation of the negative and will advance the good in him and bring out the same quality in those whom he meets while traveling the path, while at the same time dissolving the negative. Humility is service to others, service done in a humble manner and without seeking recognition. The more one serves silently and unostentatiously with love and humility, while in a smiling, eager and spiritual mood, the more quickly he opens himself to the ECK which in turn serves him.

The Milwaukee Lectures
August, 1966

189

You who feel lonely should remember that the ECK Master is always with you. To do so frees one from loneliness, unhappiness and fear. To overcome such negations, give yourself up to the ECK Master, accept him for what he is, and do as he wills. Through this process one will lose all interest in this world, except for his social duties to family and work which will be performed in all sincerity. You will be surprised at the success which comes with surrendering to the ECK Master, that Inner Master who takes care of all things for every individual chela who is under his care.

Letter to London
January, 1966

Reaching the SUGMAD is the highest goal in man's life, but it is also the most difficult. We have been oversold by the metaphysicians that life comes easy provided we seek and contact God. This is not true, for only those who are really in search of Truth should step forth on the path of ECK. All others should stay in their respective places until spiritually developed so that the ECK Master will make his appearance to each.

The Albuquerque, New Mexico Talks
August, 1966

The truth about God's interest in us is shocking. He is not at all interested in the human state, or embodiment, but only in the continuation of life. He is vitally interested in trying to get the human consciousness to open for the ECK to flow through to the outer world of matter, energy, space and time. He knows all things that go on in his worlds, including the chirp of the cricket, but He is not interested in the problems which the human consciousness makes for Itself. It is left up to us to find the solution to the condition into which we have fallen while living on this plane. It is not difficult to resolve all problems, provided we allow ourselves to follow the spiritual law and not be diverted by those who seem to be led by Kal (the negative power).

New Cosmic Star
Los Angeles, Calif.

190

No saviour who has come to this world intended, or intends, to propagate a religion. Instead he wants to relay a certain few truths learned in the spiritual kingdoms. The ancient ECK masters followed this method. They scarcely wrote anything, for few of their followers had the ability to read. They passed the message of ECK by mouth. Once they initiated one person onto the holy path, they would turn to another.

The Far Country

By desire we are bound to the objects of desire. This is why the complete detachment of the mind from every worldly object is necessary. Detachment avoids bondage to the world and its objects of the senses. If we love anything with the desire to possess it we enter into being the slave of our desire.

Dialogue in Buenos Aires
November, 1957

When one examines the spiritual values he finds that beliefs, speculations, and faiths have little to support him in the desire for immortality. All elements of the many world religions are doubtful in their value to him, because they are dependent upon ancient and modern metaphysical theories. This is what is wrong with our present teachings in the spiritual field. The values are all set wrong for they are more social benefits which are of this world than on the understanding and knowingness of the God world.

Spiritual Consultation to a chela
in India, May, 1965

Many people believe that spirituality can be gained by reading books, studying discourses and listening to a master, but this isn't true. Spirituality is caught. Once we learn the secrets of the spiritual life from an ECK Master, and have become alive with the life it generates within, we do not have to have physical contact with the Master. But we can have that inner contact — inner association with him — anywhere, and at any time.

The Bonn, Germany Talks
July, 1967

191

Many people find it difficult to believe in the ECK Master because he is not known too well among the masses. One of the strangest things about the human mind is its tendency to discredit present-day mastership and give glory to that which is ancient. The modern mind cannot accept that which is here and now before its own eyes.

Helsinki, Finland Talks
July, 1968

The fact that great spiritual travelers — the ECK Masters — have lived with us for centuries on Earth, and are here today, is one of the most important, most cheerful and most hopeful thoughts which man can have. The light of the ECK Masters is in no way dimmed by comparison with those of the ancient path. Many of the ancient masters are still living with us here on Earth.

The Far Country

Occasionally someone will report the sayings and actions of an Inner Master whom they have had for quite some time. It is true that many people do not believe in these inner ones whom they call ascended Masters. They rely mainly on these entities and never on the Master who is among them in the physical flesh and at the same time acting as the Inner Master. They can become so dependent on the so-called Inner Masters that they are introverted. They start believing they are guided by something, a higher being who gives them the right spiritual advice and leads them toward great missions. Nothing could be so wrong. This is a dangerous area to tread, for it is very easy for anyone to pass over the borderline into the paranoid state. This is what the Kal does in order to keep one within its own net. It leads people on, making them think that they are here for great missions, and gives them delusions of their own greatness. These people are often able to report hallucinations which they believe are magnificent visions sent to them especially by the Supreme Deity. All religious history is filled with the tales of these people, regardless of sect.

Dialogue in Rotterdam
July, 1968

192

We have been sold a package by the religionists that God will grant us anything in life. This is too bad, for most of us sit around with the idea that we are on a spiritual welfare program and all there is to do is to ask. God is supposedly ready to grant us such desires. This is pampering the human consciousness and deluding the public into thinking that all one has to do is to be good, hold positive thoughts and be expectant of such materialistic blessings.

I tell you, this is the worst of the so-called spiritual teachings. We can only get what is put into the spiritual life, and if we do nothing, then how in the world can we expect something? It is the old "something-for-nothing" program which is so prominent in our lives today.

Berne, Switzerland Talks
July, 1968

After one is able to leave the body daily on his own volition there is no death for him, in the ordinary sense of physical extinction or dying. Anyone using the ECK energy steps out of his body at will and in full possession of his faculties. When the time comes for him to leave his body permanently, he steps out of it as one would a prison, and goes into higher regions with the assistance of the ECK Master.

Dialogue in Rangoon
February, 1946

So many people automatically resist the ECK! They lack belief in truth, and because of this karma is always added in large quantities. When one resists the ECK Master, trouble is arising for one's self. The energy which is hostility and flows outward to the ECK Master meets with no resistance, and must return to itself. He is his own target.

Letter to a Chela in Hong Kong
March, 1965

Many aspirants seeking God are unhappy because they cannot get any degree of psychic manifestations or experiences in Soul Travel. The great problem here is that they are meeting with resistance, and completely missing the point altogether. Manifestations which include entities in the

193

field of spiritualism (I am speaking here of those who need an outside channel to make contact with the astral entities) are those concerned with the psychic. This is a problem because we are then trying to work with the point of focus, that is, the physical seat of the psychic faculties. However, some persons get mixed up because they believe that this is the spiritual faculty in the physical body. Knowing that this latter faculty is located between the eyes and is known as the spiritual they waver back and forth between this psychic seat and the spiritual seat. This confuses them and they never get anywhere with either psychic manifestations or spiritual experiences.

Illuminated Way Monthly Letter
October, 1968

Direct knowledge of God through the inner channels is the goal of every seeker of the Supreme Deity. There are many roads which lead to the divine wisdom and enlightenment. But perfection can never be gained in the human state of consciousness because only a few — and I repeat this — only a handful of the aspirants are ready for full participation in the Kingdom of God, other than those who follow ECK. Of Itself ECK is the only path which can give anyone perfection during this lifetime.

Dialogue in New York
December, 1966

Man's consciousness of himself is the foundation of his highest self. But since we have several types of consciousness, we must proceed from the highest state. This is what gives man the ability to distinguish between the inner "I" which we call Soul, and the external word or that which we call "myself." So when we begin to put such things into the consciousness as the abstracts known as beauty, goodness and love, we are only working with the human state. We are putting a distinction between good and᾿ bad, ugly and beautiful, and all the rest of the abstracts. But when we see and know only detachment from either of these states, goodness and badness and the other dichotomies, the we are in the spiritual state. When none of them affects us

194

emotionally and we can use them for our own tools, we are truly becoming candidates for the ECK initiation.

Letter to a Chela in Rome
March, 1968

When a man dies there cannot be much change in his spiritual unfoldment simply because he crosses the borders of physical death into the other worlds. He will be placed wherever the ECK Master knows he has earned in his earthly sojourn. The next dimension will be as equally limited as his state of consciousness was on this side where he was bound by customs, traditions and difficulties. His spiritual environment there will be practically the same as where he dwelled in his human consciousness. However, he does have the opportunity (as ever) to advance, because I have that ability to instruct on any plane to any ECK chela regardless of whether his environment is in the spiritual worlds, the physical plane or any of the planets.

Dialogues in Istanbul
April, 1947

"I am Always With You" is a phrase not to be taken lightly. It is true. Every ECK chela should realize this at all times: in crises, during peaceful periods, and in contemplation on the spiritual exercises of ECK.

First World Wide Seminar
October, 1967

OTHER BOOKS
BY
PAUL TWITCHELL

ILLUMINATED WAY PRESS
P.O. BOX 82388
San Diego, California 92138